The Household
of God

The Household of God

God's Pattern and Plan in Heaven, on Earth, and in the Church

William A. McKinnon

An imprint of Watchman Writer's Collective, printed and distributed by Ingram Spark Press

The Household of God
Copyright © 2021 by William A. McKinnon

All rights reserved. No part of this publication may be reproduced, stored in a retrieval system, or transmitted in any form or by any means—electronic, mechanical, photocopy, recording, or any other—except for brief quotations for printed reviews, without prior permission of the publisher.

Scripture quotations, unless otherwise noted are taken from the New King James Version of the Bible, ©Thomas Nelson Publishers, 1982.
Used by permission.

An Imprint of Watchman Writers Collective, LLC of Tampa, Florida.

Published by Ingram Spark Publishers

ISBN 9780578924960

Cover art by Susan Kerr

Printed in the United States of America

ACKNOWLEDGEMENTS

So many people have been great assets in helping and supporting me as I have labored in writing this book. First and foremost, would be my precious wife Ginger, whom I married sixty-plus years ago, and who gave birth to our four children; our firstborn, William *Billy* A. McKinnon, Jr., our beautiful girl Susan, who is married to the editor of this project. Robert McKinnon and his lovely family, and our youngest son, Fred McKinnon, whose Christian music is now being heard worldwide.

Joe Kerr edited this manuscript and has written and co-written several books and has edited books for many other writers. Several years ago, when I mentioned to him that I felt the Holy Spirit told me to write a book, but I had no idea how to do so, he simply said, "Just write! I'll help you with it." I wrote a note that said, "Joe: Just Write" and stuck it on my computer where it stayed until I finished the book. Joe also made many suggestions, which helped clarify what I was trying to convey.

I also acknowledge Pastor L.A. Joiner, now retired and enjoying life with his precious wife Teresa at Saint Augustine Beach, Florida. When I was ordained as a Pastor in our local church, which was planted by my friend, Pastor Gilbert Posey, and his wife Debi, I knew very little about pastoral responsibilities and functions. I was aware of a man named L.A. Joiner who founded the Christian Alliance of Ministries, located in Valdosta, Georgia. Though he knew nothing about me, a cousin of mine who had worked with him called him and told him a little about me. He said, "I'll be happy to meet him," and made an appointment for me to visit him at his office in Valdosta.

From that meeting forward, I have had a relationship with him that has been a tremendous blessing. Even now, many years later, when I need godly direction and counsel, he always answers my phone calls and has never failed to provide the counsel I needed. Pastor L.A. has truly been my "Spiritual Father" in my life on earth. His counsel always aligns with the Holy Scriptures. I have indeed been greatly blessed through my relationship with my "Spiritual Father," who lives on earth.

Finally, even though they have long ago gone to spend eternity in heaven, I acknowledge greatly my earthly Father and Mother. I constantly thank my Heavenly Father, who ordained I be born a son to Sarah and Andrew McKinnon and raised in such a godly environment.

My Dad taught me to be a man of my word. He also taught me that two things would bring me great harm - a pencil and a gun. I understood later in my life that this lines up with Holy Scriptures. (He further taught me that law enforcement personnel carried both!)

I also acknowledge many of my brothers in Christ. They have been great assets in providing wisdom, truth, and encouragement throughout the 31 years I have been active in some form of ministry. Twenty-one of those years, I have served as the Senior Pastor of the local assembly I helped build. One of my greatest encouragers has been my long-time friend and now an outstanding pastor himself, Stacey Stone. He calls me frequently to check on how I'm doing in the latter years of my retirement and to exhort and encourage me.

Thanks so much to Jeff and Sylvia Williams, the husband-and-wife pastoral team of Community Life Church. As a team, they are truly amazing and have encouraged me in so many ways and have blessed Ginger and me with financial offerings as well. Pastor Sylvia has also been a great help to me as I have struggled with poor eyesight, poor computer skills, and, at my age of 84, a struggle with occasional early-onset dementia.

I also acknowledge Rev. Mike Wells, currently the leader of CAM Leadership Network, located in Valdosta, Georgia. Mike has great spiritual insight, and he doesn't hesitate to speak the truth regarding what he sees and discerns in the Spirit! Mike has encouraged me and has scolded me at times, all intended to make me a better pastor and a stronger Christian. I am sure many others could have been listed here, and I apologize to any who may have been overlooked. We'll add you in the next book.

Blessings on you all!

INTRODUCTION

He was a mean man! He was a deceiver, a liar, and a thief. Jacob was his name, and the name "Jacob" literally means *Supplanter or Deceitful, One who takes the heel.* He used these characteristics to lie to and deceive his father Isaac into giving him the inheritance that legally should have belonged to his older brother Esau.

Even though the evil scheme was planned and directed by his Mother, Jacob was the one who chose to commit the deceit. Consequently, his older brother planned to kill him, which caused Jacob to flee from his homeland and spend years in a foreign land. (Genesis 27).

On the journey to the foreign land, Jacob had a dream of a ladder set up on the earth. It's top reached to heaven, and the angels of God were ascending and descending on it. The Scriptures record that the Lord stood above it and gave Jacob a promise concerning his future and how the Lord was to bless him tremendously in the coming years.

When Jacob awoke he declared, *"Surely the Lord is in this place, and I did not know it. How awesome is this place! This is none other than the house of God, and this is the gate of heaven!"* (Genesis 28: 16-17).

Jacob's deceptive nature still directed his actions in the years he spent working for a foreigner who was as deceptive as Jacob. Finally, in Jacob's final deceptive plan, he left at night, took his family and his livestock, and fled, heading back to his homeland to face the wrath of his older brother.

The ladder dream occurred during this journey, fleeing his life serving Laban. Jacob was alone and sleeping on a rock when he met *"a Man who wrestled with him until the breaking of day."*

The account continues that Jacob could not prevail against Him. During the wrestling match, the Man touched the socket of Jacob's hip, and his hip was instantly out of joint. The match was over.

He lost, but I just love the tenacity of Jacob! He would not let the Man go! Jacob persevered and even with a dislocated hip, responded, *"I will not let you go unless you bless me!"*
The Man asked, "What is your name?"
"Jacob"
The Man said, *"Your name shall no longer be called Jacob, but Israel; for you have struggled with God and with men, and have prevailed."* (Genesis 32: 22-30).

As we follow Jacob's transformation, we see that this man named Jacob, who became Israel, became one of the most powerful rulers of the Jewish leadership in the Old Testament, which is proof that God can transform anyone who commits his life solely to the Lord!

I can definitely relate to Jacob because I have had two wrestling matches with God.

Contents

The First Wrestling Match 1
The Second Wrestling Match 3
My Personal Story 9
Abiding in God's Household 19
The Nature and Characteristics of the Spiritual Household of God 28
The Titles of God 36
Abiding in God's Household 46
God's Spiritual Household 48
The Pattern of the Household of God 55
The Father Figure in the Pattern of God's Eternal Spiritual Household 78
The Holy Spirit – The Type and Shadow of a Godly Mother 80
Jesus Christ –The Firstborn Son 86
The Pattern of the Church God's Spiritual Household on Earth 95
The Pattern of the Earthly Family Household 113
A Real-Life Example of a Godly Father 121
God of Borders 126
God, the Creator 135
A Return to the First Wrestling Match 139
The Pattern Hidden and Covered 141
The Conclusion of the Whole Matter 148

The First Wrestling Match

The first one occurred on August 20, 1992, nine years after I met the Lord Jesus Christ and gave my life to Him. I received Him as my Savior and the Lord of my life at a Full Gospel Businessmen's Advance Retreat in January 1983.

A friend of mine I highly respect announced the Holy Spirit had directed him to plant a church in the small city where my family and I lived at the time.

I struggled with this concept until the Holy Spirit spoke to me and told me I should support this work. My friend became my Pastor and appointed me to Elder and Praise and Worship Leader. The church began in an upstairs room of a building on the main street of McRae, Georgia. Growth began to occur, and two years later, we purchased a larger building on the edge of town.

As the church continued to grow, the senior pastor brought in another minister to be a part of the ministry team. Things went well for a season. Then I began to observe some things that concerned me. Finally, after midnight in the early hours of August 24, 1992, I got out of bed and went outside the house to the deck began to submit my concerns to the Lord. As soon as I had made my concerns known, Jesus the Lord, the head of the church, spoke clearly to me. He said, *"I am calling you to be a pastor in this church."*

The wrestling match had begun!

Imagine my response to this shocking word. I immediately blurted out, "Lord, You've got the wrong man!' I followed that up with another point I figured He couldn't refute: I never wanted to be a preacher! I tried that a time or two, don't You remember? It fell like a lead balloon!

The Holy Spirit reminded me of a portion of the Lord's Pray in Matthew 6:10 *"Your kingdom come, Your will be done on earth as it is in heaven."* The wrestling wasn't going my way.

Finally, I conceded the wrestling match by telling the Lord that I wanted to do what He wanted me to do. I asked Him to do two things for me that would open the door for this to take place without any conflict. First, I asked God to reveal my calling to my church and that they would affirm the two ministry gifts where I was currently serving in the church.

Second, I asked Him to direct me through the Holy Spirit to deliver a *specific* word to *specific* people for that currently appointed *specific* time. The Lord God is always faithful!

On Sunday morning, January 24, 1996, I was ordained as pastor and have served in that capacity for 22 years until I retired in 2018. When I consider the time served in other areas of ministry, it adds up to 31 years. God is so good and faithful!

The Second Wrestling Match

Twelve years ago, I was reading in the book of Jeremiah, the Old Testament Prophet. In the 30th Chapter, verse 2, Jeremiah writes, *"Thus speaks the Lord God of Israel: '**Write in a book for yourself all the words that I have spoken to you.**"*

Something stirred in my inner being and hit me like a mighty punch in the belly, and I heard the Holy Spirit speak clearly, "Write a book entitled **'Household of God."**

I immediately knew He was referring to the 2nd Chapter of The Epistle of Paul, the Apostle to the Ephesians. *"Now, therefore, you are no longer strangers and foreigners, but fellow citizens with the saints and members of the **household of God**, having been built on the foundation of the apostles and prophets, Jesus Christ Himself being the chief cornerstone, in whom the whole building, being fitted together, grows into a holy temple in the Lord, in whom you also are being built together for a dwelling place of God in the Spirit"* (Ephesians 2:19-22).

The second wrestling match began with new excuses. I felt they were perfectly legitimate, and certainly, the Holy Spirit would understand.

"I've never written a book!" More wrestling.

"I don't know how to write a book!" Silence, God was listening, but still wrestling.

"I wouldn't even know how to start a book." More wrestling.

"I have no idea how to organize the chapters of a book. I am computer illiterate, and my typing speed is a minus zero!" That should do it.

Ah, I felt really relieved that I had reasoned my way out of this impossible assignment.

I was actually being disobedient to the word of the Lord. Solomon, the most intelligent man ever to walk on the face of the earth, wrote, *"Trust in the Lord with your whole heart and do not lean* on your own understanding." *In all your ways acknowledge Him, and* **He shall direct your paths.***"*

Oh, the goodness of God our heavenly Father! The Scriptures record: *"The Lord is not slack concerning His promise, as some count slackness,* **but is longsuffering toward us***, not willing that any should perish but that all should come to repentance"* (2 Peter 3:9-15).

Two years later, the Holy Spirit spoke to me again and reminded me that I need to write the book. This time I began to research statistics of our modern society. I was diligent in gathering a great amount of research, but once again got busy with being a pastor in the church. A good friend and brother in Christ made a statement that I'll never forget. He said, "If the Devil can't make you sin, he will cause you to get busy."
I confess my guilt!

Finally, in my time in the presence of the Lord shortly after retiring from being pastor of the church, I asked Him what I could do in my older age to advance His kingdom work on the earth I heard the Holy Spirit say in a very stern voice, "Write the Book!"
My response was, "Yes, sir!" Another wrestling match. The Lord, once again, the winner.

When I met the Lord Jesus and was born again in January 1983, I realized the importance of knowing the word, will, and way of God the Father, God the Son, and God the Holy Spirit.

I knew it was essential that I spend time reading the Scriptures because the absolute eternal truth, the very word of the living God, is recorded there. Consequently, I have read the Bible from Genesis to Revelation many, many times.

I truly believe with my whole heart two portions of Scripture. The first is from 2 Timothy 3:16,17: *All Scripture is given by inspiration of God, and is profitable for doctrine for, for reproof, for correction, for instruction in righteousness, that the man of God may be complete, thoroughly equipped for every work."*

The second is found in Hebrews 4:12,13: *"For the word of God is living and powerful, and sharper than any two-edged sword, piercing even to the division of soul and spirit, and of joints and marrow, and is a discerner of the thoughts and intents of the heart. And there is no creature hidden from His sight, but all things are naked and open to the eyes of Him to whom we must give account."*

Because I believe God's Word is powerful and has absolute authority, I have included many Scriptures in this book, and I make no apologies for doing so.

I strongly encourage the readers to read, pray over, and apply these holy truths in their walk with God the Father, God the Son, and God the Holy Spirit. Most of the Scriptures used are taken from The New King James Version of The Holy Bible. Other translations will be noted.

We will cover numerous topics throughout the book. Still, all will relate in some way back to the foundational principle, **Abiding in God's Household.**

We will examine the absolute eternal truths concerning who the builder of this house is, the character and nature of God, the different names of God, including the Hebrew names that portray His redemptive power. Finally, we will discuss how we can apply that Bible knowledge to our place in the Household of God, both eternally and here and now.

We will also cover the current culture of our lifestyle and beliefs in the United States of America and how it reflects our viewpoints concerning the plans and purposes of an Eternal, Almighty God. We will also investigate the status of the church in America. Throughout the book, I've included many testimonies from different viewpoints to give the reader a complete picture concerning these topics.

I have also included documented research, which reveals the current mindset of our society. Much has changed in the way our society thinks and consequently how our current worldly belief system has led many astray from the Word of God. We will examine our worldview – what it is and what it should be according to God's purpose and plan for humanity.

Other subjects presented in the book include the liberty we have been given to choose for ourselves, the power of our choices, and the consequences our choices produce.

Satan is the enemy of God. His greatest effort is to cause the children of God to doubt our beliefs and ignore the word of God! After my salvation I realized that in order for me to grow in the spirit I had to fully believe and commit to being a "doer" of His word as recorded in the Holy Bible. The Apostle, warns his readers by writing: *"But be*

doers *of the word, and not hearers only,* ***deceiving yourselves.*** *"* (James 1:22).

Consequently, I made it my goal in life to establish a lifestyle of reading the Scriptures daily so His word would be in my heart and mind. The psalmist writes: *"Your word I have hidden in my heart, so that I might not sin against You."* (Psalm 119:11). Therefore, any word preached, and "sayings" heard, and any thoughts that enter my mind I immediately test to see if they line up with the written word of God!

Immediately after Jesus was baptized in the Jordon River by John the Baptist and was recognized as the Son of God by the Father's voice from heaven and the Holy Spirit's descending upon Him in the form of a dove, was let into the wilderness by the Spirit to be tempted by Satan.

After forty days of fasting and prayer, Satan came to tempt Him. In every instance, Jesus answered the temptation by quoting the Word of God. Satan finally left Him with the intent of tempting Him further later in His life. Jesus always defeated the enemy with the Word of God!

Jesus Christ is our pattern, and to be victorious in our spiritual warfare, we must always compare what the Word says with the ideas or thoughts Satan uses to assail us. We cannot win these battles without knowing what is written in the word of God.

We need a mindset change. I can think of no better word on that than the absolute eternal truth for a mindset change revealed under the inspiration of God through Paul's letter to the Romans.

Paul writes: *"**And do not** be conformed to this world, but be **transformed** by the renewing of* *the mind, that you may prove what is that good and acceptable and perfect will of God"* (Romans 12:2).

As we begin, hear God's promise to His children as recorded in Psalm 92:12-15:

"The righteous will flourish like a palm tree, and grow like a cedar in Lebanon. **Planted in the house of the Lord,** *they will flourish in the courts of our God. In old age they will still bear fruit; healthy and green they will remain, to proclaim, 'The Lord is upright; He is my Rock, and in Him there is no unrighteousness.'"*

My Personal Story

I was born and raised in a godly family and taught the ways of God by my father and mother. There were six children in the family: five boys and one girl. We were members of a little country church, and our parents carried us to every service held there.

My father was a farmer and a businessman, and we worked hard and played hard. My job during my youth was to bring in the firewood that had been cut and split so it could be used for cooking and warming the house.

At age five, I milked my first cow. We used the milk for drinking at meals and for making butter. My older brother and I would soon be milking two or three cows early every morning before the school bus came and again late in the afternoon.

This was during the early stages of World War 2. I remember the days of food rationing when families were issued rationing coupons to purchase essential food from the country store.

My dream was to be a cowboy. Even when very young, I would blanket and saddle my bedstead and pretend to be riding a horse. The day came finally when one Christmas morning I found a saddle, cowboy boots, a cowboy hat, and a little cap pistol under the Christmas tree.

My Dad suggested I go outside where he had tied a pony, my first. I was ecstatic!

Eventually, my Dad gave me the job of looking after the cattle he owned, and the pony was traded for a real quarter horse.

Dad wanted the cattle checked twice a day, once in the morning before I went to school and then later when I got home from school. During these times, I learned how to lasso calves and cows to be treated for insect infestation and worms. Those were some of the best days of my life growing up as a young man.

Since I had become the cowboy of my dreams, my next desire was to begin competing in rodeos. My Dad said, "Absolutely not. It's too dangerous."

Nonetheless, when I went to college, my friend and I decided we would start entering the rodeos held in our state. Disobedience, however, has a way of being exposed at some time.

At my very first rodeo, I won second place in the calf-roping event. I was unaware that some friends of my parents saw the write-up in their local newspaper, which listed the winners. They thought Mom and Dad would be proud of their son, so they mailed them the article.

After receiving the article, Dad called me at college. I still remember the call: "Bill, I want you to come home this weekend."

Still naive, I hitchhiked home that weekend. My Dad wasted no time getting right to the point. He told me that he and Mom didn't want me to compete in rodeos but that if I wanted to do it so much, they would agree under one condition. I must agree to let them know where and when I was going to be at the next rodeo so they could pray for me and that I'd let them know how it went.

Eventually, I got permission from the officials at the University of Georgia to move my horse to the University farm. From there, my friend and I became regular rodeo contestants every weekend and worked rodeos in Georgia, Alabama, and North and South Carolina. I used my winnings to help pay my way through college.

After graduation, I wanted to rodeo all the time. This time Dad took a stand. He firmly told me I was to get a regular job that had a good future for me. I was disappointed but realized his wisdom. Shortly after that, I interviewed and was hired as an assistant County Agent in Cordele, Georgia, with the University of Georgia Cooperative Extension Service.

The first Sunday I was in Cordele, I went to the Cordele First Methodist Church for their morning service. As the service began, I noticed this young brown-eyed brunette in the choir. My heart skipped a beat!

The next Sunday morning, I was back in my seat at the same church.

Following the service, a man introduced his daughter to me – Ginger, the same beautiful brown-eyed girl from the choir.

This was in the middle of September. We had our first official date on Valentine's Day the next year. We were married the following June.

I had promised myself that due to the dangers involved in rodeos, I would quit the sport after I got married. Consequently, prior to our marriage, I sold my beloved horse, my saddle, and all the tack I had accumulated over the years.

After four years of service in Cordele, where two of our children were born, I accepted the offer to move to Telfair County Georgia as the County

Extension Director. That is where our other two children were born and where I retired after thirty-one years of service.

During this time, we were very active members of the United Methodist Church in McRae, Georgia. We are extremely blessed to have four children, three grown boys and one girl, all happily married, thirteen grandchildren, and two great-grandchildren. We recently celebrated our 58th wedding anniversary!

We are very blessed; however, I began to drift away from the Lord in the earlier years. The things of the world caught my focus. 1 John 2:16 states: *"For all that is in the world - the lust of the flesh, the lust of the eyes, and the pride of life - is not of the Father but is of the world."*

My focus was drastically wrong, and I found myself living an ungodly life that led to alcoholism and adultery. I began having thoughts of suicide, primarily because of a bad business decision which left me with a debt of over half a million dollars.

It was about this time in my life that my older brother Jim began to talk with me about a group of men called the Full Gospel Men's Fellowship (FGMF). He had been attending some of their meetings and was amazed at the miraculous things that were happening during these meetings.

Jim had been struggling with issues in his own life, and I had noticed a drastic change in the way he had overcome these issues. He told me about Annual Men's Advance, an annual meeting the FGMF held at the Rock Eagle 4-H Club Center in Eatonton, Georgia, in January every year. He invited me to join him and some men from Mount Paran Church of God in Atlanta.

I had no desire at all to accept his offer, so I kept putting it off with any excuse I could dream of. Finally, he called to say the deadline for registering was at hand, and he needed to know whether to include me.

My response was to go ahead and register me. I figured if I didn't go, I would repay Jim the cost of the registration and that would be that.

Surprisingly to me at that time in my life, I found myself packed and headed to the Men's Advance on Friday afternoon in January 1983. Not knowing what to expect, I stopped by a liquor store and bought a bottle of Scotch to carry with me.

Upon arrival, I registered for the weekend and was assigned to stay in a cabin with 12-14 other men. As other men began to arrive, I observed them getting out of their vehicles, shouting, "Hallelujah, Praise the Lord!" I thought to myself, "What in the world am I doing here? These guys are crazy!" They were literally *running* to meet other men and, of all things, men hugging men!

I felt like I was at a crazy house! Yet, at the same time, I sensed these guys had something I hadn't seen in a long time. They were joyously excited and happy to see each other.

The thought crossed my mind, "Is this the love of God that I've read about and heard preached? Could this be the real thing? They seem to be genuinely excited and so happy to be here." I decided I would hang around and see what was next to come.

The first night's service, I was both fearful and expectant at the same time. There were over 400 men in the building. The service started with praise and worship, a totally new experience for me.

The praise and music began to slow down and get quieter. Suddenly a man in the back of the room stood and began to speak in a language I had never heard. My thoughts began to jumble over each other. "This must be those 'tongues' I've heard about. He does not even have a microphone, and yet I can hear him clearly. It's a beautiful language. You just can't learn that language!"

As soon as he stopped speaking, another man stood and gave what I have since learned was interpreting the first man's language. Simply put, it was the word of God directly spoken to me. Things were said that no one but God and I knew anything about.

Dr. Mark Rutland, one of the most powerful evangelists I have ever heard, delivered the message that followed. I don't really recall the context of the sermon, but I will never forget the question he posed at the end of the message: "If you're not 100% sure you are saved, you are lost!"

Even in my corrupt situation, I thought, "I *think* I am." As if he heard me, Dr. Rutland said, "If you're thinking, 'I *think* I am,' you are lost!"

He was not reading my mind, but there was no doubt the Holy Spirit had revealed what someone present was thinking. It was decision time. I turned to my brother and said, "I don't know about you, but I am going to get this dealt with right now!"

The fact of the matter is, I didn't even go up to the altar to be prayed for. I just quietly and privately bowed my head and met the Carpenter of Nazareth - the risen Lord and Savior - face to face. I opened my heart to Him and asked Him to come into my heart and be the Lord of my life.

Something powerful happened, and I was instantly changed and born again, becoming a new creation in Christ (2 Corinthians 5:17). I kept my poor brother and his friends from Mount Paran Church awake most of that night, asking questions about the Bible, God, Jesus, and the Holy Spirit. I'd never been so hungry to learn more about these things.

The rest of the weekend was awesome. Men were giving their lives to the Lord Jesus, and miracles were being manifested. Men shared testimonies about being saved and living in Christ.

There was great praise and worship. I couldn't keep my hands from lifting up to praise my Lord. After the retreat ended on Sunday afternoon and the whole drive back home, I knew I was a changed man, and that nothing would stop me from growing in the Spirit and becoming a disciple of the Lord.

When I returned home from the Advance Retreat my precious, godly wife asked me, "How did the weekend go?" I began to try to tell her what happened. Every time I tried to talk all I could do was cry! Formally, in my adult life I had cried only one time, and that's when my favorite dog Caleb who had been my constant companion for years had to be put to sleep because of heartworm infestation.

Finally collecting myself, I was able to say, "The next time they have one of these Advances I want you to go with me." It wasn't long before a big meeting was held nearby. This time wives were invited, and Ginger got her first taste of what I had experienced earlier.

Even though I knew I was a changed man I was still drinking heavily. I didn't know much about who the Holy Spirit was or what His function in the life of a Christian was, but in my private prayer time I would constantly ask Him to be involved in my life, especially my desire to be free of alcohol.

The next year I recruited several men to go with me to the Men's Advance in January of 1984. Following each service there were usually two altar calls – one for salvation, and the other for the baptism of the Holy Spirit. I went forward to receive the baptism of the Spirit. Although someone prayed for me, I sensed no change at the time. Still hungry for all the Lord had for me, I kept praying for the baptism of the Spirit.

I'll never forget the Saturday morning three months later. I was sitting in my County Agent's office filling out some reports that were due the next week. Since it was Saturday, I was in the office alone. Suddenly the Lord spoke very clearly to me. *"Bill, you can't be the man I need if you have a glass of liquor in your hand!"*

Immediately I pushed all the paperwork aside and responded: "Lord, I want to quit drinking! I have tried to quit many times and have not been able to! However, I want what You want more than anything else, so the next time I feel like I've got to have a drink I'm going to look to You and give my problem to You."

Something powerful took place in the realm of the Spirit at that moment. I was filled with the Holy Spirit, and instantly delivered from the bondage of alcoholism! The desire for a drink was still heavy on me for a time, but from that day forward I have not had a drink of liquor, and that was 35 years ago! Oh, the goodness of God, and the power of the Holy Spirit!

My life was totally changed. Like a man nearing starvation I was hungry for the word of God. I immersed myself in the Scriptures, and have read the Bible through many, many times. I attended church services anywhere I could hear the word of God proclaimed. I was witnessing to men every day and was leading others to the Lord Jesus daily.

I was also diligently looking for what I called a "Full Gospel" church to join. However, God had a different plan. He instructed me to stay in the denominational church where I had been raised. Along with my wife and family, we stayed there for two more years and saw a great deal of fruit produced while we were there.

Throughout those days, my four children were watching me closely. It was like the old country saying, "They were looking at me like a cow looks at a new gate."

They had seen me get caught up in other things like hunting, fishing, and hobby projects. I guess they thought that's what this new spiritual life was. However, as time went by, they decided what I had was genuine, and one at a time each one of them have been saved, giving their lives to Jesus the Lord, and are all following Him rigorously.

That's the greatest blessing a father who loves his children can have! We will shift from earthly fathers to heavenly Father and back again throughout the book, but I wanted to establish a few applications and illustrations for later chapters.

You will read about my father, and his father, and the profound impact of both on my life and family. I love how God creates our story which He then uses to create His-story - the history of fathers and households.

Abiding in God's Household

"Now, therefore, you are no longer strangers, but fellow citizens with the saints and members of the household of God, having been built on the foundation of the apostles and prophets, Jesus Christ Himself being the chief cornerstone, in whom the whole building, being fitted together, grows into a holy temple in the Lord, in whom you also are being built together for a dwelling place of God in the Spirit." **(Ephesians 2:19-22)**

Wow! What an awesome vision for those of us who have really become a new creation in Christ (2 Corinthians 5:17).

In this next few chapters, we are going to study the household of God; what it means, how it works, and how it affects our everyday life.

First, God Himself is the builder of this household. We find this eternal truth in the Book of Hebrews, emphasizing the faithfulness of Abraham. Chapter 11:9-10 reads, *"By faith he dwelt in the land of promise as in a foreign country, dwelling in tents with Isaac and Jacob, the heirs with him of the same promise; for he waited for the city which has foundations, whose **builder and maker is God.**"*

Our heavenly Father is one part of the Triune Godhead. God the Son - Jesus Christ the risen Lord and Savior, the Father, and God the Holy Spirit, all work together to build an amazing and awesome home for those who have received salvation through faith in Jesus Christ and His finished work on the cross. In the following pages we will delve into the many facets of God's supernatural divine household.

We will focus on His pattern and plan for life, and what He requires of those who are members of His holy house. We will also examine our natural households in this life on the earth and how they line up with the requirements of His household in the spirit.

We want to be thorough and exact in our search, so we will examine the status of our current day's culture as detailed in the statistics revealed by well-known research reports from highly respected sources both religious and secular. Stay with me, and I believe we'll all be shocked at how things have changed in our current society.

The culture I was raised in has changed so drastically since I was born and raised in a godly household in the mid-thirties. Perhaps you've lived longer, perhaps not as long. Either way, looking at these changes, it behooves us to question the future of life on this earth in the years to come.

Our basis for this comparison will be the absolute, eternal **truths** revealed in Holy Scripture – the very Word of God.

When I refer to the **facts,** I am referring to the world's belief system. What the world believes is their worldview. It is revealed in the American society we live in today – a secular worldview.

These **facts** represent **truth** to the society as they see and understand it. Yet these facts are primarily the reasoning of the carnal man's mind. In reality, these ideas and thoughts absolutely do not line up with the eternal truth recorded in the Holy Scriptures – a Christian worldview. This Spiritual blindness is what Paul described in 1 Corinthians 2:14 when he explained "The natural man (unsaved) does not accept the things that come from the Spirit of God. For they sound like foolishness to him and he cannot understand them because they are spiritually discerned.

We will review these facts compared to the eternal, spiritual truths contained in the Word of God. As we study together, I encourage you to read and re-read the Old Testament book of Judges.

Remember this truth: when God created mankind, He gave humanity the freedom of choice. Every choice we make produces a consequence. Most good choices produce positive consequences, while bad choices can often produce negative consequences. This principle is clearly manifested in the Book of Judges.

Consider this Word of the Lord from Judges: *"In those days there was no king in Israel; everyone did what was right in his own eyes."* (Judges 17:6; 21:25). Another reference puts it this way: *"There is a way that seems right to a man, but its end is the way of death."* (Proverbs 14:12). These verses describe individual choices, but the results can affect an entire nation, as we repeatedly see happen in Judges.

Webster's Dictionary defines the word **Individualism** as follows: (1) "A doctrine that the interests of the individual are or ought to be ethically paramount; conduct guided by such doctrine. (2) The concept that all values, rights, and duties originate in individuals."

Webster defines the word **Relativism** this way: "The doctrine that knowledge, truth, and morality exist in relation to culture, society, or historical context, and are not absolute."

I recently attended a meeting of a coalition of ministers from several states. A good friend of mine and a brother in Christ, Rev. Mike Wells, who pastors two churches in South Georgia and oversees this coalition of churches, spoke at this particular meeting.

He made a statement that witnessed very strongly with my spirit: "We live in a post-modern society which has moved from the objective, verifiable truth that governs society as a whole, to creating their own truth; a subjective, unverifiable reality which only concerns them or their world view. The foundation of truth has been eroded slowly and methodically by sin, resulting in Relativism."

Did you hear the subtle hiss of the devil in that? The doctrine of *Relativism is a belief* that knowledge, truth, and morality exist in relation to culture, society, or historical context and are not absolute. This concept is absolutely a lie from Satan himself!

Consider the absolute, eternal truth of an almighty, holy God as recorded in the First Epistle of Paul the Apostle to the Corinthians, verses 18-25. God says, *"I will destroy the wisdom of the wise, and bring to nothing the understanding of the prudent."* (Verse 18). Verse 25 reads: *"Because the foolishness of God is wiser than men, and the weakness of God is stronger than men."*

Why then does the current culture in our nation so dominate our lifestyle?

Let's refer again to the absolute eternal truth of God. In 1 Corinthians 2:14, it is written, *"But the natural man does not receive the things of the Spirit of God, for they are foolishness to him; nor can he know them, because they are spiritually discerned."*

The conclusion is that some live according to the current culture that has moved from the objective, verifiable truth to one that creates its own truth, a subjective, unverifiable reality that only concerns them or their worldview.

In other words, they tell themselves, "Others are living this way, so it must be right." Or, to put it more simply, if it feels good, do it.

My heart grieves for the many people who live that life, for they are definitely not members of the Household of God!

I am often told that I should, *"Judge not, that you be not judged"* (Matthew 7: 1).

Indeed, those were the very words of Jesus the Lord. But it's dangerous to base theology on one verse of Scripture; rather, we should always base our theology on the full word of God.

For instance, the word 'judge' literally means *condemn*. Let's verify this concept with the words Lord Jesus says in John 7:24, *"Do not judge according to appearance, but judge with righteous judgment."*

Let's examine another concept on the subject of judgment spoken by the Lord Jesus concerning false prophets. In Matthew 7:17-20, we read Jesus' words, *"Even so, every good tree bears good fruit, but a bad tree bears bad fruit. A good tree cannot bear bad fruit, nor can a bad tree bear good fruit..."* (verse 20) *"Therefore **by their fruits you shall know them.**"*

Consequently, when people throw out that one phrase: "Judge not that you be not judged..." my response is that I'm not a judge; I'm just a fruit inspector.

The fruit I observe in the lifestyle of our current culture is quite often directly opposed to the truths outlined in the Scriptures and can be viewed as anti-Christ because they violate the very laws of God and His commandments.

Many of the people who follow our current cultural lifestyle are members of the Church who claim to be Christians.

When asked the question, "Do you believe in God," they would give a resounding, "Of course I believe in God!" But is belief enough? Consider the word of the Lord in the Epistle of James, *"You believe that there is one God. You do well. Even the demons believe and tremble!"*

For example, our current culture believes it is completely normal to have a sexual relationship before marriage. Many couples move in together and live a life as husband and wife before marriage. The Lord God calls this adultery, and adultery is sin in the eyes of a holy God.

In the Apostle Paul's letter to the Romans, he writes: *"For the wages of sin is death, but the gift of God is eternal life in Christ Jesus our Lord."*

Let's look at the absolute truth of the Word of God in another Scripture, Galatians 5:16-21. Paul makes a clear distinction between being led by the Spirit and being led by the lusts of the flesh.

In verse 19, he lists adultery as one of the works of the flesh. Then in verse 21, Paul writes, ***"those that practice such things will not inherit the kingdom of God."***

We find strong confirmation of this truth in 1 Corinthians 6:9-10: *"Do you not know that the unrighteous will not inherit the kingdom of God? Do not be deceived. Neither fornicators, nor idolaters, nor adulterers, nor homosexuals nor sodomites, nor thieves, nor revilers, nor extortioners **will inherit the kingdom of God.**"*

Furthermore, the writer of Hebrews states, *"Marriage is honorable among all, and the bed undefiled, but fornication and adulterers God will judge"* (Hebrews 13:4). God's Word is consistent.

I love being in the presence of the Lord. One early morning a few months ago, I was reading the Bible and noticed two passages in the same chapter of the Gospel according to Matthew, one of the 12 Disciples of Jesus.

In these two passages, Jesus is giving counsel concerning eternal life and the only way to receive it. Jesus makes this absolute statement:

*"Enter by the narrow gate; for wide is the gate and broad is the way that leads to destruction, and there are **many** who go in by it. Because narrow is the gate and difficult is the way which leads to life, and there are **few** who find it."* (Matthew 7:13-14).

Seven verses later Jesus says, *"Not everyone who says to Me, 'Lord, Lord' shall enter the kingdom of heaven, but he who **does** the will of My Father in heaven. **Many** will say to Me in that day, 'Lord, Lord, have we not prophesied in Your name, cast out demons in Your name, and done many wonders in Your name?' And then I will declare to them, 'I never knew you; depart from Me, you who practice lawlessness!'"* (Matthew 7:21:21-23)

These verses really caught my attention. As I continued to search the Scriptures, I discovered a similar passage in the Gospel of Luke. Jesus used a different term to convey this same eternal truth. Jesus responded to a question from a man in Jerusalem, *"Lord, are there **few** who are saved?"* Jesus responded by saying, *"Strive to enter through the narrow gate, for **many**, I say to you, will seek to enter and **will not** be able"* (Luke 13: 23-24).

Fearing the Lord is not a bad thing. If we love the Lord and desire to make Him the Lord of our life, it's a very good and holy thing.

As I read the above verses, the fear of the Lord came all over me. The Psalmist records, *"The fear of the Lord is the beginning of wisdom; A good understanding have all those who do His commandments. His praise endures forever"* (Psalm 111:10). Many, few… what does that mean?

I searched Strong's Concordance to find out the Greek meaning of the words **many** and **few**. The word **many,** used as a noun, is translated, "Much, abundance, plenteous, or the large majority."

The word *few*, when used as a noun, is defined this way, "A small number of units or individuals; a special limited number."

When used as an adjective, Strong's defines *few* as, "Consisting of or amounting to only a small number; at least some but indeterminately small in number." If this doesn't stir the fear of God in you, I am concerned on your behalf!

The good news of the Gospel is, there is always hope!

Romans 5:5 tells us that hope does not disappoint. If we are truly members of the God's Household, we may know, *"what is the hope of His calling, what are the riches of His glory, and what is the exceeding greatness of His power toward us toward us who believe, according to the working of His mighty power"* (Ephesians 1:18-19).

There are so many Scriptures that promise us hope. Launch a study of the word hope, and you will begin to understand you don't need to live a hopeless life, for if Christ is in you, He is the hope of glory. (Colossians 1:27)

Always remember: *The Lord is not slack concerning His promise, as some count slackness, but is **longsuffering toward us, not willing that any should perish but all should come to repentance***" (2 Peter 3:9).

The Nature and Characteristics of the Spiritual Household of God

If we desire to be members of God's household, there are certain things we must understand about who God really is. We need to know what His nature and plans are for the members of His household. And we need to know what we must do as our part of the covenant to become a member of His divine, eternal household.

In the Book of Proverbs, Solomon, the wisest man on the earth, writes this: *"It is the glory of God to conceal a matter, but the glory of kings is to search out a matter"* (Proverbs 25:2).

1 Peter 2:9 is written to those of us who are truly born again Christians who have yielded our lives to serve Jesus the Lord; it says, *"But you are a chosen generation, a royal priesthood, a holy nation, His own special people, that you may proclaim the praises of Him who called you out of darkness into His marvelous light; who once were not a people nut are now the people of God, who had not obtained mercy but now have obtained mercy."*

This portion of Scripture is verified in Revelation 1:6, where it says, *"...and* [Jesus] *has made us kings and priests to His God and Father, to Him be glory and dominion forever and ever. Amen."* Do not be deceived!

We will never experience the fullness and wholeness of God in this life on earth. I feel bad for you if you have fallen for the lie that you can live your best life here and now. If this life is the best you have to look forward to, you need to understand more about our eternal household in heaven!

We will live our best life, but only when we meet Him in eternity. However, through prayer and study of His word, we can uncover a lot of truth about who He is and what His nature and characteristics are.

While we cannot cover all of the nature and characteristics of God here, we will examine some of the most important. Those characteristics give us an idea of how He builds and rules His household.

1. God is **Holy**

Webster's Dictionary defines the word *holy* this way: sacred, worthy of adoration or veneration; spiritually whole, worthy of unimpaired innocence or proved virtue; godly."

In The Third Book of Moses, Leviticus, God Himself speaks to Moses and says, *Speak to all the congregation of the children of Israel, and say to them: 'You shall be holy, for I the Lord your God am holy'"* (Leviticus 19:2).

The Old Testament prophet Isaiah records a vision where he saw the Lord sitting on a throne, high and lifted up, and the train of His robe filled the temple. Above the throne stood seraphim angels. Each angel had six wings: with two, he covered his face, with two, he covered his feet, and with two, he flew. And one cried out to another and said: *"Holy, holy, holy is the Lord of hosts; the whole earth is full of His glory!"* (Isaiah 6:1-3) Numerous other verses confirm God's holiness.

Not only is God holy, but as an essential requirement of being a member of His household, we must also be holy.

In fact, Hebrews 12:14 states that we should *"Pursue peace with all people, and **holiness**, without which, **no one will see the Lord.**"*

Sounds totally impossible, doesn't it? However, keep this eternal truth in your heart and mind - our God is a God of Love, and He never requires anything of us that He has not already made provision for us to do!

The key to this provision appears in Colossians 1:27, *"To them* (those who abide in Christ Jesus) *God willed to make known what are the riches of the glory of this mystery among the Gentiles: which is **Christ in you**, the hope of glory."*

Let's examine the provisions of God to those who are members of His household. It all begins with the process of our salvation. Ephesians 2:8-10 reads, *"For by grace you have been saved **through faith,** and that not of yourselves; it is the **gift** of God, **not of works**, lest anyone should boast. For we are His workmanship, created in Christ Jesus for good works, which God prepared beforehand that we should walk in them."*

God has given us grace - the enabling ability and power of God, the Holy Spirit. He has also given us the gift of faith. In Hebrews 11:1 we read what faith is. *"Now faith is the substance (realization) of things hoped for, the evidence (confidence) of things not seen."*

Furthermore, the moment we accept Jesus Christ as the Lord of our lives, all things become new. *"Therefore, if anyone is in Christ, he is a **new creation**; old things have passed away; behold **all things have become new.**"*

Let's focus for a moment on the seemingly insignificant two-letter word, '**if.**'

This little two-letter word is a conditional word. It appears in the Bible 1,521 times, 1,029 times in the Old Testament, and 492 times in the New Testament. This same two-letter word is implied in many other places throughout the Bible. It simply means that **if** we do what God commands us to do, He will absolutely do what He says He will do. WOW!

However, **if** we don't do what He asks us to do, we essentially tie God's hands and disable Him from fulfilling His covenant promises.

We serve an amazing and powerful God. We read about the Israelites in Psalms 78:40-41 while they were in the wilderness: *"How often they provoked (rebelled against Him) in the desert! Yes, again and again, they tempted God, and **limited the Holy One of Israel**."* Not a good thing to do!

Consequently, **if** we are truly "born again" (John 3:1-8) we live, move, and have our being in Christ Jesus.

In Colossians 2:9, Paul the Apostle, under the anointing of the Holy Spirit, writes: *"For in Him dwells all the fullness of the Godhead bodily (in bodily form) and you are **complete** in Him, who is the head of all principality and power."*

As a final touch, when we are baptized in the Holy Spirit - also known as the Spirit of Grace - the very ability and powerful nature of God that raised Jesus Christ from the grave inhabits us.

We are equipped and powered to do the works of Christ on the earth today as He did while on the earth in bodily form (John 3:12-13.). And yes, we can indeed live holy lives on this earth.

2. God is **Love**

Everyone who knows anything about God probably knows or has heard John 3:16,17. John quotes the Lord Jesus:

"For God so loved the world that He gave His only begotten Son, that whoever believed in Him should not perish, but have everlasting life. For God did not send His Son into the world to condemn the world, but that the world through Him might be saved."

God's love flows from His heart, which desires that through Jesus Christ, all have the opportunity to be saved and delivered from an eternity in hell. In the 14th chapter of John, Jesus said, *"I am the **way**, the **truth,** and the **life**. **No one comes to the Father** except through Me."*

Simply put, life in Christ Jesus, with a genuine demonstration of His works through the individual, is the only way to insure life eternally in the presence of a holy God.

God's love for the whole world is so pure and holy that He is *"longsuffering toward us, not willing that any should perish but that all would come to repentance"* (2 Peter 3:9).

God always confirms His Word. It is written in 1 John: 4:8-9: *He who does not love does not know God, for **God is love.** In this the love of God was manifested toward us, that God has sent His only begotten Son into the world, that we might live through Him."* The love of God is unconditional. We cannot earn His love.

In Romans 2:4, we read the following: *"Or do you despise the riches of His goodness, forbearance, and longsuffering, not knowing that the goodness of God leads you to repentance?"*

I have heard people say that God is too busy to be concerned about them and their problems. What a lie from the devil!

Consider God's statement from Jeremiah 29:11: *"For I know the thoughts I think toward you, says the Lord, thoughts of peace and not of evil, to give you a future and a hope."*

Let's look at the same passage of Scripture from The Message translation: *"This is God's word on the: subject: 'As soon as Babylon's seventy years are up and not a day before, I'll show up and take care of you as I promised and bring you back home.* ***I know what I'm doing.*** *I have it all planned out - plans to take care of you, not abandon you, plans to give you the future you hope for. When you call on Me when you come and pray to Me, I'll listen."*

He loves us as we are, but He is a holy God who has certain definite requirements we must meet if we are to become a member of His household. These requirements will be outlined and discussed in a later portion of this book.

3. God is a **God of Wrath**

In many churches, as well as in sermons preached on television, we hear much about the love of God. It is rare, however, to hear sermons preached on the wrath of God.

When I began to enter the calling of the Lord as a pastor many years ago, the Holy Spirit led me to a portion of Scripture in James chapter 3, verse 1: *"My brethren. Let not many of you become teachers, knowing that we shall receive **a stricter judgment.**"*

I have held this truth in my heart and on my mind ever since. Paul the Apostle clearly expresses the essence of this truth in Romans 1:16,17: *For I am not ashamed of the Gospel of Christ, for it is the power of God to salvation for everyone who believes, for the Jews first and also for the Greek. For in it, the righteousness of God is revealed from faith to faith; as it is written, "The just shall live by faith."'*

Consequently, the members of the church I pastored - World Outreach Church - will verify that I have ministered on the wrath of God several times over the years.

As we study the word of God in the Holy Scriptures, we find many Scriptures that address this side of God the Father's nature.

I recommend reading Psalm 2:1-5. Pay attention to verse 5, where it is written: *Then He (God) shall speak to them in His **wrath**, and distress them in His deep displeasure."*

In the 95th Psalm, God is grieved (disgusted) with the Israelites because they went astray in their hearts and did not follow His ways. God says in verse 11: *"So I swore in My **wrath**, 'They shall not enter My rest.'"*

The Apostle Paul writes in his letter to the church in Rome: *"For the wrath of God is revealed from heaven against **all ungodliness and unrighteousness** of men, who suppress the truth in unrighteousness, because what may be known of God is manifest in them, for God has shown it to them"* (Romans1: 18-19).

Finally, **God is a God of Many Names.** God, our Heavenly Father, is known by many names in the Bible, not because the writers didn't know who He is, but because they wanted to explain Him in all the glory and majesty they could imagine, but it was a huge task for any language.

God's character is so comprehensive that He cannot be defined unless we understand each of those names. Each one unlocks another revelation of who He is and how He functions. All of the names reveal His full nature.

To fully understand His nature and His ways, we will look at a brief list of the names He is known by in Scripture. We will discuss each of them in more detail. There are many others, but we will focus on six names.

Using personal testimonies, we will see how God reveals His character and nature through His names. As we begin to comprehend His names, we will see why each is used, and what they mean to us. If we understand who God is and see His person and nature and character, we can understand how we are to live our lives so we can daily abide as members of His holy household.

God reveals His nature and His love in His names. When we understand those names, it gives us a greater understanding of His character and nature. With that understanding, we have access to His awesome power. That power – His power – empowers us to live as members of His household on earth—the Household of God.

The Titles of God

The titles of God are different from the names of God, which we will discuss later. The titles identify a function of His being God. The names explain who He IS, His essence and the core of what makes Him the eternal Almighty God.

1. God of Creation

In Genesis 1:1 we read: *"In the beginning, God created the heavens and earth."*

As we continue reading in Genesis, we discover that we are created in God's image. We are image-bearers of God Almighty. *"And God said, 'Let us make man in Our image, and after Our likeness'"* (Genesis 1:26,27).

We see the Trinity in creation where it says *"Let **Us** make man in **Our** image..."*

Hebrews 11:3 says that God spoke and the worlds were created: *"By faith we understand that the universe was created by the word of God. So that what is seen was not made out of what is visible."* The world and everything in it came into existence by God's command—the Word of God.

John established Jesus as the functioning operator of creation because Jesus is the Word. John 1:1-3 states, *"In the beginning was the Word, and the Word was with God, and the Word was God. The same was in the beginning with God. All things were made by Him, and without Him was not anything made that was made."*

Paul confirmed this truth to the Greeks on Mars Hill, *"...for in Him we live and move and have our being, as some of your own poets have said. 'For we are also His offspring'"* (Acts 17:28).

2. God of Purpose
In Ecclesiastes 3:1 it is written: *"To everything, there is a season, a time for every purpose under heaven."*

God's purposes are rarely made evident to us according to our timing because God is timeless. However, God manifests His purpose according to His own wisdom and love toward us.

Describing God's purpose, the Apostle Paul writes, *"But when the fullness of the time had come, God sent forth His Son, born of a woman, born under the law, to redeem those who were under the law, that we might receive the adoption as sons"* (Galatians 4:4,5).

God's timing is always impeccable. The heart of God is always focused on us individually because He has a specific purpose for everyone born on the earth.

Consider that God knows each of us before our time begins. Before we are born. Before we are conceived. Before Earth existed, God knew us.

*"...according to the power of God, who has saved us and called us with a holy calling, not according to our works, but according to His own purpose and grace which was given to us in Christ Jesus **before time began.**"* (2 Timothy 1:9).

Grasp the powerful truth and significance of this absolute eternal truth - the holy God of love knew us before time even began. He created us individually and had a divine purpose for us before we were even born!

For example, in my life, God's holy calling before time began was for me to minister as the Pastor in the local assembly known as World Outreach Church. However, the fullness of time for me to enter into that calling came fifty-five years after my birth.

God knows what He's doing. In his letter to the church in Rome, Paul wrote: *"And we know that all things work together for good to those who love God, to those who are called **ACCORDING TO HIS PURPOSE.**"*

As we examine Paul's letter to the Ephesians, we get an idea of one thing all who are in Christ must do as His children on earth. This one thing is a requirement of abiding in His household.

In chapter Romans 2:10, Paul writes: *"For we are His **workmanship, created in Christ** Jesus for **good works**, which God prepared beforehand that **we should walk in them.**"*

Finally, let's examine the word of God as written in The Revelation of Jesus Christ, Chapter 17:17: *"For God has put it into their hearts to **fulfill His purpose,** to be of one mind, and to give their kingdom to the beast until the words of God are fulfilled."*

God has a purpose for everyone, even for those *"who dwell on the earth whose names are not written in the Book of Life from the foundation of the world."*

Hear me now. There will be a payday one day. Those who have not surrendered their hearts to the lordship of Jesus Christ will still, one day, bow before Him and profess He is Lord and Savior.

However, their confession will come too late. They will be assigned to eternity in hell with

Satan and his army where there is no presence of God. His love and light are absent.

Think about this: Our awesome, holy God, Who is not bound by time, can do everything simultaneously because time obeys Him, not the other way around. Thus, our Creator can think about us all the time. I encourage you to keep in mind a Scripture I have quoted earlier where God speaks concerning the way He thinks about us.

Jeremiah wrote: *"For I know the thoughts I think toward you, says the Lord, thoughts of peace and not of evil, to give you a future and a hope."*

3. God of Patterns and Plans

The nature of God as a God of patterns and a God of plans is an interesting but very vital concept we must be aware of and agree with if we are to become a people who are qualified to abide in His holy household.

As we examine the word of God, we begin to get a clearer picture of how our Holy God designs His household.

God made this very clear to the Israelites after He delivered His people from the slavery and oppression of the Egyptians and Pharaoh through His servant Moses.

Under the rule of this evil Pharaoh, the Hebrew children grew in numbers into a great nation. Pharaoh understood that if they continued to grow, their sheer numbers might eventually challenge his kingdom. So, Pharaoh made them his slaves, forcing them into great oppression.

They began to cry out to God for deliverance. God heard their prayers and sent His servant Moses to deliver them.

Pharaoh refused, so God sent ten plagues against the Egyptian nation. Pharaoh still resisted until the tenth plague - the death of every firstborn child and livestock of the Egyptian nation. The Israelites were exempt from all the plagues.

After the tenth plague, Pharaoh finally relented and released the Hebrews. In addition to freedom, God gave the Hebrews favor with their Egyptian slave lords. Their taskmasters gave them food, gold, clothing, and other valuable items. The Hebrews plundered the Egyptians.

While on their journey to the Promised Land God had chosen for them, they camped on the edge of the Red Sea to rest and offer sacrifices to the Lord who had delivered them from Egypt. Meanwhile, Pharaoh became angry and ordered his army to follow and destroy the Hebrews. Pharaoh himself accompanied the army to see that the mission was successful.

The Hebrew children became fearful and cried out to God. God heard their cry and commanded Moses to raise his staff over the sea. When he did, the sea split open, allowing the Israelites to cross over to the other side on dry ground. When Pharaoh and his whole army tried to cross over in pursuit, God released the waters, and Pharaoh and his entire army were drowned!

4. God of Order and Structure

We will talk about Jehovah Jireh The God Who Provides in a later chapter more application for us in this age. Here, we want to look at the Jehovah Jireh in His relationship with Israel.

During their journey to the Promised Land, the Israelites had to go through a wilderness. Their journey went through many miles of desert where there was no water.

They complained and even grumbled they wished they were back in Egypt, where water was abundant. Then they observed the works of Jehovah Jireh. God, their Provider, instructed Moses to strike a rock with his staff. When Moses obeyed, water gushed out of the rock! Jehovah Jireh provided.

Another time, there was no food available. Again, Israel complained against Moses and God, grumbling that they always had food back in Egypt.

The Psalmist Asaph reports: *"How often they provoked Him in the wilderness and grieved Him in the desert! Yes, again and again, they tempted God and limited the Holy One of Israel"* (Psalm 78:40-41).

Nevertheless, our longsuffering and patient God heard their cry and sent fresh manna down from heaven every morning, and when they complained because they wanted meat, He sent down quail as a source of meat. Suffice it to say, the Hebrew children recognized the might and power of God and wanted Him to dwell with them.

Moses interceded for the people, and God spoke to Moses. God told Moses if they built Him a Tabernacle, He would abide in their presence. Then God called Moses to the top of the mountain, where He showed Moses the Tabernacle in Heaven.

God, the Creator and Builder, commanded Moses to build the Tabernacle according to the pattern of the one in heaven. God insists that His pattern be followed in His holy household on earth as well.

"And let them make Me a sanctuary (sacred place) *That I may dwell among them. According to all that I show you, that is, the **pattern** of the*

*Tabernacle and the **pattern** of all its furnishings, just so you shall make it"* (Exodus 25:8-9).

In verse 40 of the same chapter, God reminds Moses: *"And see to it that you make them* (the articles in the Sanctuary) *according to the **pattern** which was shown you on the mountain."* God reiterates His command in the 26th chapter when He says to Moses: *And you shall raise up the tabernacle according to its **pattern** which you were shown on the mountain."*

As we continue to follow the building of the Tabernacle, we see a holy God Who strongly insists on following His pattern. He directs Moses how the interior of the tabernacle should look (in this case, regarding the altar of burnt offerings).

God tells Moses: *"You shall make it hollow with boards; as it was shown you on the mountain, so shall they make it"* (Exodus 27:8).

Let's move forward through the Scriptures to the point where the Tabernacle has been erected. All things are arranged as God commanded, and we see the importance of following His instructions. You may be wondering, "Why does God care about building design and architectural plans?"

There is a much larger principle at work than mere construction design. God's power is released when we follow God's **pattern** for His household.

In this instance, following God's plans for the Tabernacle empowered the place to release God's provision for the Land for Israel. There is power in the Household of God. When we follow His plans, His provision follows.

In Exodus, Chapter 40:33-34, we read: *"And he* (Moses) *raised up the court all around the tabernacle and the altar, and hung up the screen of the court gate. So, Moses finished the work. Then the cloud covered the tabernacle of meeting, and* **the glory of the Lord filled the tabernacle. And Moses was not able to enter the tabernacle of meeting because the cloud rested above it, and the glory of the Lord filled the tabernacle.***"* What an awesome sight this must have been!

Some reading this book might be thinking, "Why is this important? This is old covenant stuff." Paul discussed just how important that old covenant stuff is in his first letter to the Corinthians.

Paul notes that there is power in following those examples. 1 Corinthians 10:6 states, *"Now these things became our examples, to the intent that we should not lust after evil things as they also lusted."* Furthermore, Paul urges the Philippians toward obedience when he writes: *"Brethren, join in following my example, and observe those who* **walk according to the pattern** *you have in us."*

The writer of Hebrews reminds us of God's word to Moses about building the Tabernacle, *"See that you make all things according to the* **pattern** *shown you on the mountain"* (Hebrews 8:5).

Let's leave the Israelites and Moses and move forward in time to King David's days. God's chosen servant David wanted to know God's heart. David had a great desire to build a temple, a permanent place for God's presence to abide. However, God told him that since he was a warrior who had shed the blood of many of his enemies, he could not build the temple.

1 Chronicles 28:6 records this statement from David, *"Now He* (God) *said to me, 'It is your son Solomon who shall build My* **house and My courts;** *for I have chosen him to be My son, and I will be his Father.'"*

Reading further in this same chapter, note David's instructions about following God's pattern. David instructs his son Solomon in verses ll-12a, *"Then David gave his son Solomon the **plans** for the vestibule, its houses, its treasuries, its upper chambers, its inner chambers, and the mercy seat; and the **plans** for all that he had by the Spirit, of the courts of the **house** of the Lord, of all the chambers all around, of the treasuries of the **house** of **God**, and of the treasuries for the dedicated things."*

Note that the word **pattern** has now changed to **plan**. God has a pattern *and* a plan. We cannot put God in a box. He is much too big for us to limit Him.

As I write this, I remember my younger days when some of my friends thought it was great fun to call the small grocery stores in the area and ask this question about a popular cigarette tobacco: "Do you have Prince Albert in a can?" Of course, they did; it was the preferred tobacco for rolling cigarettes in those days.

When the store's owner answered the phone, he would usually respond by saying, "Of course I do!" At that point my friends would say, "Well open it up and let him out!" Then they would quickly hang up the phone.

How often do we restrict a holy God by limiting Him with our own thoughts and desires? It's time to allow God to be the amazing powerful God who wants us to yield our own personal thoughts, ideas, and plans to His.

The wisdom of God is clearly stated in Proverbs 3:5-6: *"Trust in the Lord with all your heart, and **lean not to your own understanding. In all your ways** acknowledge Him, and **He shall direct your paths.**"*

The choice is ours to make. Just remember that a good choice produces a good consequence while a poor choice produces a poor consequence. His good plans and our choice to follow equals His power in the functioning Household of God.

Abiding in God's Household

All who earnestly desire to abide in God's Household, both in this life on earth and forever in eternity, must fully accept the absolute eternal truth that God is a God of order. He has a specific pattern and plan for how His household is to be ordered and operated. Not everyone who desires to abide in His household will do so.

Allow me to give a personal illustration: My wife Ginger and I are blessed by God us to be the parents of four children, three sons and one daughter.

Suppose that when they were young children living in our home, I was asked to allow a pedophile to move in with us and become part of our family.

I love people, which is God's commandment for me to love Him with my whole heart, and to love others as myself (Matthew 22:36-40). But because I am required to protect me household, I make choices with them in mind.

A lawyer of the Pharisees asked Jesus a question to test Him, saying, *"Teacher, which is the greatest commandment in the law?' Jesus said to him, 'You shall love the Lord your God with all your heart, with all your soul, and with all your mind. This is the first and great commandment. And the second is like it: You shall love your neighbor as yourself. On these two commandments hang all the Law and the Prophets.'"*

I not only believe these words of Jesus, but also put them in practice in my everyday life. In obedience to that verse, I would do everything in my power and ability to help this young man who is a pedophile to get the right counsel and help he needs to be delivered and healed from an abominable lifestyle.

However, to protect my family, I would never let him move into our household. In the same way, I truly believe God would not allow sinners who refused to repent of their sins and become changed by the power of faith and the grace of God through the work of the Holy Spirit to abide in His Holy household.

God's Spiritual Household

The basic requirements for eligibility to become a resident in God's household are clearly revealed as we invoke the help of the Holy Spirit to diligently search the Scriptures. Just as God spelled out His requirements for the Tabernacle and Temple, He will reveal His purpose and plan.

God's household has certain residency requirements. In many ways, these requirements compare with the natural household I was raised in. We will compare God's requirements and those you and I can observe over the years in the households of families in America and draw some conclusions.

I begin with the very first household established when God created the heavens, the earth, and all they contain.

In the first chapter of Genesis is a recording of all the animals, birds, and other living creatures, which God created.

Verses 26-28 read: *"Then God said, 'Let Us* (God the Father, God the Son, and God the Holy Spirit) *make man in Our image, according to Our likeness; let them have **dominion** over the fish of the sea, over the birds of the air, and over the cattle, over all the earth and every creeping thing that creeps on the earth.' So God created man in His own image; in the image of God He created him, **male** and **female** He created them. Then God blessed them, and God and said to them, 'Be fruitful and multiply; fill the earth and subdue it; have dominion over the fish of the sea, over the birds of* *the air, and over every living thing that moves on the earth.'"*

Up to this point, when God observed the things He had created the Scriptures quote Him saying: *"And God saw that it was good."*

Fast forward to the verse 31 where it records God creating man and woman: *"Then God saw everything He had made, and indeed **it was Very good....**'"* [emphasis added]

Pay special attention to God's creation of mankind. He created **male** and **female – a man and a woman.**

I heard this saying many years ago: "God created Adam and Eve, not Adam and Steve." A culture, which believes it's acceptable for parents of a household to be either two men or two women simply cannot be considered as those who qualify for abiding in God's household, for homosexuality is an abomination to a holy God!

For further examples of those not eligible as members in God's household, I refer you to Galatians, five, verses 19-21 where the Apostle Paul writes about the works of the flesh and states emphatically, *"...those who practice such things will **NOT inherit the kingdom of God."***

As we moved forward in examining the essential requirements for abiding in God's household, please understand these requirements are based on three different concepts: the Spiritual household, the Natural Household, and the Church - the flesh and bone body parts of Jesus Christ.

We will also examine the requirements essential for every member of the household we discuss. The Spiritual household requirements are clearly outlined in the Holy Bible, as are the natural family requirements. We will discuss the individual requirements of each member of the household, also found in the Scriptures, a little later.

Since I was blessed to be born a son in the natural household of Andrew and Sarah McKinnon, I will use my natural household as an example. Your experience may be different, but I consider my household fairly normal, so I will use it as a reference point. Your experiences may be different from mine, but most of the points will still apply.

Let's consider first the Spiritual Household of God. We stated earlier that God Almighty Himself is the designer and builder of His Holy Household. He has built His House by laying the chief Cornerstone, Jesus Christ the Lord and the only begotten Son of God.

I refer you again to the John 3:16-17: *"For God so loved the world that He gave His only begotten Son, that whoever believes in Him should not perish, but have everlasting life. For God did not send His Son into the world to condemn the world, but that the world **through Him** might be saved."*

The foundation is the most vital element in the construction of any building. I will discuss this topic a bit later in this book; now however, let's examine the other stones of the household of God.

Jesus Christ the Lord is the (1) **Chief Cornerstone!** Keep that eternal truth in mind. It is the foundation in more ways than one.

The writer of Hebrews, addressing spiritual immaturity, writes this: *"Therefore, leaving the discussion of the elementary principles of Christ, let us go on to perfection* (maturity)*, not laying again the **foundation** of (2) repentance from dead works and of 3) faith toward God, of (4) the doctrine of baptisms, of (5) the laying on of hands, of (6) the* *resurrection of the dead, and of (7) the eternal judgment"* (Hebrews 6:1-2).

Many years ago, I was in my "outdoor office" - a place located in the woods fairly close to my Pastor's office at the church I was serving. Any time I felt the need to escape the strife and pressure I was in at the time I would go to this secret place and get in the presence of the Holy Spirit and commune with Him.

On one such day, I was searching the Scriptures seeking further confirmation concerning the foundation stones of the Household of God. The Holy Spirit led me to Proverbs 9:1, *"Wisdom has built Her house, She has hewn out her **seven pillars;**"* Praise God! He **always** confirms His holy word with other Scriptural references!

One more final confirmation of this eternal truth is recorded in the Matthew 16:13. There we find a dialog between Christ and His disciples. It begins with Jesus asking His disciples a question, *"Who do men say that I, the Son of Man, am?*

The disciples responded by telling Jesus what the people were saying about Him. Then Jesus asked the disciples another question – one that each of us must answer eventually: *"**But who do you say that I am?"***

I just love the apostle Peter! He is so bold, brash, and open, even sometimes when he is totally off base. Yet, hear his response to Jesus' question: *You are the Christ, the Son of the living God."*

Note Jesus' response to Peter: *"Jesus answered and said to him, Blessed are you, Simon Bar-Jonah, for flesh and blood has not revealed this to you, but My Father who is in heaven. And I also say to you that you are Peter, and on this rock, I will build My church, and the gates of Hades shall not prevail* (be victorious) *against it. And I will give you the keys of the kingdom of heaven, and whatever you bind on earth will be bound in heaven, and whatever you loose on earth will be loosed in heaven"* (Matthew 16:13-19).

It's vital that we understand exactly what Jesus was saying to Peter and the other disciples. He was not speaking of building His Church on Peter, the disciple, as some misunderstand that statement. Christ said He could build on the **divine revelation** Peter had received from God the Father through the Holy Spirit – that Jesus is the Christ.

Consequently, this same truth of divine revelation through the Holy Spirit must be the way we live and move and have our being to be eligible to be a member who abides in His household.

The Lord Jesus Christ spoke these words while He was on this earth, *"Therefore whoever hears these sayings of Mine, and **does them,** I will liken him to a wise man who built his house on the rock: and the rain descended, the floods came, and the winds blew and beat upon the house; and it **did not fall**, for it was founded on the rock. But everyone who hears these sayings of Mine, and **does not** do them, will be like a foolish man who built his house on the sand: and the rain descended, the floods came, and the winds blew and beat on that house; and it fell. And great was its fall"* (Matthew 7: 24-27).

The Apostle John quotes Jesus where He states a promise followed immediately by another promise, which gives us great hope. Jesus says, *"These things I have spoken to you, that in Me you may have peace. In the world you will have tribulation; but be of good cheer, I have overcome the world"*

Praise the living God that He has made provision for us daily to live fruitful and productive lives even amid the challenges and tribulations we face daily in this life.

As we begin to examine the spiritual household of God, I am aware that many who read this book may not be familiar with some of the terminology I will be using, especially as it relates to two words: **Type** and **Shadow**. So, let's define those words.

Romans 5:14 reads, *"Nevertheless death reigned from Adam to Moses, even over those who had not sinned according to the likeness of the transgression of Adam, who is a **type** of Him who was to come."*

In the Epistle of James, he uses the word '*similitude*' (meaning *likeness*) instead of **type** (James 3:9). The word '**shadow**' is utilized in two places in Hebrews, Chapter 8, verses 4-5, and chapter 10 verse 1. It is the same concept.

It means something that resembles the original, like a print of a famous work of art—there is only one Mona Lisa painting, but you can buy an original print. It may be the same in all regards, size, canvas, and color. It is not the original, but it looks the same.

The writer combines the two words, '**Copy**' **(Type)** and '**Shadow**' when he writes: *"For if He (the High Priest) were on earth, He would not be a priest, since there are priests who offer the gifts according to the law; who serve the **copy** and **shadow** of the heavenly things, as Moses was divinely instructed when he was about to make the tabernacle. For He said, 'See that you make all things according to the **pattern** shown you on the mountain.'"* In Hebrews 10:1, the writer states,

*"For the law, having a **shadow** of the good things to come, and not the very image of the things, can never with the same sacrifices, which they offer continually year by year, make those who approach perfect."*

Finally, in Paul's letter to the Colossians, he writes: *"So let no one judge you in food or in drink, or regarding a festival or a new moon or Sabbaths, which are a **shadow** of things to come, but the substance* (literally *body*) *is of Christ"* (Colossians 2: 16-17).

The Pattern of the Household of God

God's pattern for His household is clearly outlined in the Holy Scriptures and is meant to be followed in each of the three structures we will examine: The Eternal or Spiritual Household, the Natural Household of mankind on earth, and the pattern and organization of the Church on Earth.

Since each of these is meant to be a copy and shadow of God's eternal household, we will begin there.

In the pattern or plan of His holy household, there are specific requirements that are essential for the whole household to be complete and in order; for the entire household to be healthy, godly, and blessed by God.

Let's examine each of the positions and compare them to the other two – the natural human household and the structure and order of the Body of Christ—God's Church on earth.

1. God's eternal holy household

The father of this household is God the Father Himself. We must be aware of the truth that God the Father is known by many names with each name revealing His specific nature and purpose.

We discussed earlier a few of God's Old Testament names, but there are many more.

Depending on the context of the book, chapter, or verse, God is called: *El Shaddai* - God the Almighty; *Elohim* - God the Creator; or *Jehovah* - God the Lord.

Jehovah refers to God's relationship with humanity—He is our Lord. There are ten different variations of Jehovah in the Old Testament. To conserve time and space, we will examine only six of them - the names known as **the Redemptive Names of God.**

Redemption is the release of a hostage or prisoner upon the receipt of ransom. We were redeemed when Christ died for us; He paid the ultimate price. These seven names show the love that God has for us, that He would allow the ultimate sacrifice of His Son's life. (1 John 4:10).

Psalm 23 illustrates all seven of the qualities of the Redemptive Names of God. Let's begin there.

Jehovah is proper name for the Lord God. In Hebrew, it is often a prefix and not a complete name. God's name was so holy, the Hebrew scribes substituted the title YHVH (Hebrew has no vowels, only consonants) which later became Yahweh.

That was translated to Greek and Latin as Jehovah, the name of exultation establishing God almighty as Lord, God of heaven and earth, Creator, holy and eternal. The Hebrew word el was used for any god, including false gods such Baal, Ashtoreth, and others. In some verses, God Almighty is also called El saying He is THE God above all gods – the El Who is above all other els.

Each of the other names we will examine will incorporate the official title name of God, *Jehovah*, combined with a descriptive Hebrew term defining some quality or attribute of God. These are not all of the names of God, but they represent those most commonly used throughout Scripture.

1. Jehovah-Jireh is the Lord that sees and provides.

The first mention of Jehovah-Jireh in the Bible appears in Genesis 22:14 *"And Abraham called the name of that place Jehovah-Jireh: as it is said to this day, in the mount of the Lord it shall be seen."*

God is still the Lord that sees and provides. In Philippians 4:19, we read: *"And my God shall supply all your need according to His riches in glory by Christ Jesus"* (Matthew 6:31-33).

Shortly into my walk with the Lord, after I was saved and became so in love with the Lord, I entered a personal and powerful relationship with Jehovah-Jireh. Look again at 2 Corinthians 5:17 *"Therefore, if anyone is in Christ, he is a **new creation**; old things have passed away; behold, **all things have become new**."*

For me, this happened back in 1983, and, as I have also recorded in my personal story, I was deep in debt nearly three-quarters of a million dollars. I was about to lose everything I had worked for. It was at this time I met Jehovah-Jireh. Although I realize this will be a rather lengthy section, I feel compelled to share this powerful testimony. I pray it impacts you as it did me.

I was so hungry to know more about the kingdom of God that I would attend any service, which contained any ministry about God the Father and God the Son, Jesus Christ. I also searched the Christian programs on TV. One particular evening my wife Ginger and I were searching the channels and came across the "700 Club" program for the first time. We watched it with great interest.

During one part of the program, Mr. Pat Roberson and some of his staff gathered around a table to pray. They would pray out loud for a short time, then begin to share prophetic words they had received from the Holy Spirit while praying.

Suddenly, Pat Roberson looked up and pointed his finger directly into the camera. It seemed to me his finger was about two feet long. He said something like this: "There is someone watching this program that is in deep problems financially, and God says to tell you He is beginning to help you get out of debt."

The only way I can describe what happened next is to say I felt like something or someone kicked me very hard in my belly! I turned to my wife and said loudly, "That's us!"

I was an avid fan of entering the Publisher's Clearing House Sweepstakes (PCHS) in those days. I hoped I would win a big cash award. During the PCHS, I'd rush to meet the mailman each day and look for my winning announcement. However, that was not God's plan for helping get us out of debt.

Shortly after we saw the program, I received a letter from the Internal Revenue Service. I was nervous, even knowing that my CPA was an honest and good man who had filed the tax return on my behalf. With great fear and trembling, I tore open the letter.

As I slowly read the letter, my fear turned to disbelief. The letter stated that the IRS had begun a four-year investigation of my tax returns, and they found I had overpaid my taxes that first year and were enclosing a check (not a small one either) to reimburse the overpayment. What excitement and how grateful my wife and I were!

We began to thank and praise our heavenly Father for His provision. I carried that check with me that evening when I met with my fellow brothers in Christ. We were meeting each evening after work to prepare the building where the new church was being birthed.

They rejoiced with me, and I told them that I was in faith for another check in the mail the next day. Sure enough, another letter came the next day with another check in it.

Again, I shared this with my brothers in Christ and declared that I was expecting another letter and check the next afternoon. But I was wrong that time. The next day I received not one but two checks in the afternoon mail.

Honestly, I have never heard of that happening to anyone else. I know, without doubt, that was *Jehovah-Jireh*, the God who provides, working on my behalf.

Simply put, I just don't believe in coincidences anymore. I believe and receive God's word and His promises. It is the goodness and provision of God on display—Jehovah Jireh at work. I have said several times ministering to the church I would later pastor, "You can't convince me coffee is not real, because I drink a cup or two every day!"

Since those days, I've written about my Jehovah-Jireh experiences and His mysterious and mighty handiwork in my finances. I take great joy in testifying about His mighty hand at work in my finances. Bear with me as I share other testimonies of His faithfulness.

The IRS refunds were not sufficient to pay off the great financial debt I owed. However, I have much more to share of the activities and works of *Jehovah-Jireh*, God my Provider.

I'm fully aware there are those reading this book who may not accept as truth the following illustrations. Nonetheless, it is an illustration and testimony of the awesome and mysterious work of Jehovah-Jireh in my family's financial recovery. I can assure you, those who know me know I am a man of integrity who does not lie or stretch the truth. These stories are true.

During those days, I was still employed by the University of Georgia as a County Extension Director. All staff members were paid only once a month, and it was difficult for me to make all payments necessary to meet the expenses that a family of six required, even after adding my wife's meager wages.

My plan for the monthly bills was fairly simplistic: first, I would pay the essential bills (Mortgage, Utilities, etc.) that simply had to be paid. When I had done that, realizing there was not enough to pay the rest of the bills, I would often put most of what was left into our recently opened Tithe Account.

I had been raised in a godly home where we were taught as children to give ten percent to the church, save a little, and leave the rest for what we needed individually. Of course, this training had not been carried out for the rest of my adult life.

After I was saved and accepted the Lord in my heart, I remembered what I was taught and began to deposit ten percent of my monthly salary into our Tithe Account. One day the Holy Spirit simply said to me, "God does not withhold anything from you."

As I thought about this, I understood that my employer was required to withhold retirement funds, life, and health insurance funds, etc., from my monthly paychecks, so what I was receiving was only the net amount.

I thought to myself, "Holy Spirit, are You telling me I'm supposed to be giving ten percent of my gross pay to our tithe account?"

I don't know about you, but in my relationship with the Holy Spirit, I have learned that when He doesn't respond to my question, it's because He knows it was a foolish question.

We began - in faith - to deposit 10 percent of our gross income into our Tithe Account. We set a goal to give twenty percent to the Lord's work.

All the honor, glory, and praise go to the Lord, but we have maintained that level ever since. We regularly exceed that with financial gifts to others who have financial needs! I have concluded that you simply cannot out-give the Lord God!

Now, let me continue with the miraculous and mysterious work of Jehovah-Jireh in these early years of our lives. Previously, I outlined the plan I had for paying monthly bills.

At the beginning of each month, I would have a stack of bills that I had not paid, and the new bills would cause the pile to grow, yet the paycheck was the same amount. I still followed my payment plan. The month came when I started paying the bills as usual, but I was surprised to notice that I still had a balance in my checking account once I had all the bills paid.

I reviewed my math, and the balance seemed right. Since Ginger was the local bank manager, she dealt with money and balancing accounts every day. I called her and told her my problem. I stated that all the bills, both past due and currently due, had been paid, yet I still showed a surprising balance in my checking account. I was certain there must be an error in my figuring.

I asked Ginger to check my additions and subtractions because I must have made a big error somewhere. She went through my figures very carefully several times and told me there was no error anywhere. I was dumbfounded, to say the least. Immediately, I began to thank God, our Jehovah-Jireh, and to praise and worship Him.

This sort of thing has been quite customary since those days. Over and over, I have paid all the bills and still had a nice balance in my Checking Account at the end of the month - enough to deposit money in our Savings Account.

For many years now, we are debt-free and able to take a nice vacation each year. In addition to that, we have had our home of fifty-one years completely renovated, which we paid for out of our Savings Account. God is so good! He pronounces blessings unending on those who are faithful and obedient to His pattern and plan.

I encourage all who are reading this book to hear the Word of God concerning disobedience. *"Has the Lord as great delight in burnt offerings and sacrifices, as in **obeying** the voice of the Lord? <u>Behold, to **obey** is better than sacrifice</u>, and to **heed** than the fat of rams. For **rebellion is as the sin of witchcraft,** and stubbornness is as iniquity and idolatry"* (1 Samuel 15;22).

Simply stated, God loves obedience and hates disobedience. Finally, this command of God, which I seek diligently to do every moment of every day, contains both His command and His promise.

One of the most important things I seek to do daily, is recorded in Proverbs 3:5-6, *"Trust in the Lord with all your heart, and lean not on your own understanding; In all your ways acknowledge*

Him, and He shall direct (make smooth or straight) *your paths."* Honor Him, and He will honor you!

2. Jehovah-Rapha is "the Lord Who heals and restores our soul."

When the children of Israel were in Egyptian captivity, God sent Moses to deliver them. It took a series of pestilences and plagues - the final one being the death of the oldest son in every family - to convince the Pharaoh to release the Israelites.

We discussed earlier how, during these devasting plagues, the Hebrews were protected by God and were exempt from every plague.

After the Hebrew people were set free by the hand of God and led through the wilderness by Moses, the Lord God spoke this promise to Moses, *"If you diligently heed the voice of the Lord your God and do what is right in His sight, give ear to His commandments and keep all His statutes; I will put none of the diseases on you which I have brought on the Egyptians. For I am the Lord who heals you."* [Jehovah-Rapha]

In the Fall of 2011, I was seeing a specialist who dealt with men's health. After some tests, his diagnosis was that I had prostate cancer. He had already scheduled me for visits to radiation specialists and surgeons who dealt primarily with removing the prostate gland.

My wife was with me, and we looked at each other with concern. However, we were diligent in agreeing before we made any decisions. I replied to the specialist's comments by saying something like this: "Doctor, we are believers in the living God and will first seek His counsel in this matter. Then we will notify you of our decision."

On our forty-five-mile ride back to our home, we prayed together, and both of us agreed to trust Jehovah Rapha, God our healer, and believe in faith for His healing.

We also decided to limit the number of people we would tell. We would ask our children to pray with us and not tell anyone else. We also told the elders in the church I was pastoring and asked them the same thing we asked our children. All understood and agreed.

You might be wondering why we took this approach. The Scriptures state, *"Death and life are in the power of the tongue, and those who love it will eat its fruit"* (Proverbs 18:21). We knew that people like to gossip and spread bad news, and we didn't want people pronouncing death over me.

All those we trusted and knew to be powerful intercessors agreed. Finally, I called the specialists I was scheduled to see and canceled our appointments. I do not recommend this approach for everyone, but we knew it was right for us.

When I was diagnosed with prostate cancer in the Fall of 2011, my PSA was almost 7 (normal is 0-4 ng/ml). The next meeting with the doctor was in the Spring of 2012. At that visit, my PSA level tested at 4.8. Every test afterward, the PSA was down from the previous test.

The doctor's assistant would come in to deliver the report, and he would say, "I don't know what you're doing, but whatever it is, keep doing it." That opened the door for us to tell him of our faith in God the Healer, Jehovah Rapha.

In January of 2014, the PSA level had dropped to 2.9! When Jesus was facing death on the cross for our sins, He was brutally beaten with a cat-of-nine-tails whip. Most of the beatings were directed on His back.

Peter wrote about how Jesus took our punishment in 1 Peter 2:24 *"...who Himself bore our sins in His own body on the tree, that we, having died to sins, might live for righteousness – **by whose stripes** (wounds) **we were healed.**"*

Notice that the term 'were.' It indicates the past tense and confirms that healing is available today; they *were* healed. It's already done.

This eternal truth is confirmed by God's prophetic word in the Old Testament (Isaiah 53:5) and several New Testament references (Hebrews 9:28; Romans 7:6). Praise the Living God, Jehovah-Rapha, that His healing virtues are available to us today and forever.

A short time later, I shared my testimony with the church members during a sermon, and they all rejoiced with me. That was only the beginning.

In a small town like ours, word spreads rapidly. I soon received a phone call from a brother in Christ I had known for a long time. He was a member of another church in town and called to ask if he could come by my office and talk with me.

An appointment was made, and he confided to me that he had heard of my testimony. He told me he had recently been diagnosed with a similar problem and asked if I would pray for him.

I was accustomed to praying for people at the drop of a hat. Many times I have dropped the hat myself and seen God do miraculous works.

I know that *"God shows no partiality"* (Acts 10:34), so I prayed in faith for God to heal this man just as He had healed me. Not long after that, this brother came back to my office, rejoicing that his condition had been supernaturally healed, and he was free of any cancer!

He also informed me that he would tell any other victims who might have the same diagnosis to come to me for prayer, and God would heal them. I record this incident with absolutely no intention of pride or bragging, but so all the praise, honor, and glory goes to God! He is still Jehovah-Rapha, and He always will be.

Please allow me to offer a simple and short heads-up concerning praying for the sick, but one that needs vital understanding. Faith must be activated by both the one praying and the one receiving the prayer.

When we are born again and receive the Lord Jesus into our hearts, He comes by faith and through grace. The faith we have is a gift from God (Ephesians 2:8), *"Faith is the substance* (the realization) *of things hoped for, the evidence* (confidence) *of things not seen"* (Hebrews 11:1).

Our faith is activated by our belief in the Word of God, written in the Holy Scriptures.

There have been times when I was in faith, praying for healing for others who had requested prayer when I could strongly sense the person being prayed over was not activating any faith at all concerning their part in the prayer. I have observed that I have not sensed or observed healing to follow in most of these settings.

At times I have felt, "What's the use in praying for people like this?" Yet, even in those times, I have obeyed because the Lord specifically told us that we should pray for the sick. *"Confess your trespasses to one another, that you may be healed.* **The effective, fervent prayer of a righteous man avails much"** (James 5:16).

Evidently, where hidden sin has not been confessed and forgiven by God, the odds of being healed are remote, but God is always the final word. He can heal anyone and often does simply to prove Who He is and what He wants to do.

3. Jehovah-Tsidkenu is a name for God the redeemer, or the Lord our righteousness.

Jeremiah 23:6 records, *"In His days Judah shall be saved, and the Israelites shall dwell safely; and this is His name, whereby He shall be called,* **THE LORD OUR RIGHTEOUSNESS."**

Just how does this redeeming nature of God apply to those who are reading this book? Is He the Lord our Righteousness for all who have truly received Jesus as their Lord?

Put quite simply, Yes! One of God's redeeming gifts is when He gives us new birth. It is not our righteousness that saves us. It is His.

Consider Romans 3:21-22, *"But now the righteousness of God, apart from the law is revealed, being witnessed by the Law and the Prophets, even the* **righteousness of God,** *through faith in Jesus Christ, to all and on all who believe. For there is no difference."*

One of my many favorite verses in the Bible is written by Paul in 2 Corinthians 5:17, *"For He* (God) *made Him* (Jesus) *who knew no sin to be sin for us, that we might become* **the righteousness of God in Him."**

What an awesome, powerful God! He alone is love. All who come to Him through Christ Jesus by the leading of the Holy Spirit will be born again, becoming new creatures. Paul assures us the "old will pass away and **all things will become new**" (2 Corinthians 5:17).

All this and the other redemptive names of God are covered in the 23rd Psalm, written under the anointing of the Holy Spirit by David the shepherd boy and King who had an awesome relationship with God the Father.

David was known as a man after God's own heart. In this 23rd Psalm verse 4, David writes, *"Yea, though I walk through the valley of the shadow of death, I will fear no evil; for You are with me; Your rod and Your staff, they comfort me."*

The Lord *Jehovah-Tsidkenu* is the Lord our righteousness. We will discuss this further later, but consider the conversation between Jesus and Peter. It is Peter's bold confirmation recognizing that Jesus is God. By referencing this ancient name of God, Peter is stating that Jesus deserves the same *Jehovah-Tsidkenu* title.

"You are the Christ, the Son of the living God." Jesus answered and said to him, "Blessed are you, Simon Bar-Jonah, for flesh and blood has not revealed this to you, but My Father who is in heaven. And I also say to you that you are Peter, and on this rock, I will build My church, and the gates of Hades shall not prevail against it."

4. Jehovah-Shalom means the Lord of My Peace.

If we have peace, we will never fear any evil. Judges 6:2 reads, *"Now Gideon perceived that He was the Angel of the Lord. So, Gideon said, 'Alas, O Lord God! For I have seen the Angel of the Lord face to face.' Then the Lord said to him, 'Peace be with you; do not fear, you shall not die,' So Gideon built an altar there to the Lord, and called it* **'The–Lord–is–Peace.'** *To this day, it is still in Ophrah of the Abiezites."*

There are so many places in the Scriptures that refer to the term *peace*. I urge you to search the Scriptures on peace. A deeper understanding of God's peace will change the way you live.

One of my many favorite peace passages is found in Philippians 4:4-7. I have often quoted this passage when counseling with members of the church I pastored - precious men and women who were struggling to find peace in their lives: *"Be anxious for nothing, but in everything by prayer and supplication, with thanksgiving, let your requests be made known to God; and the **peace of God**, which surpasses all understanding, will guard your hearts and minds through Jesus Christ."*

Through our fifty-eight years of marriage, my wife and I have agreed that when we face a big decision, we will both pray about what decision we should make.

If we do not both have peace about our proposed decision, we simply will not move forward. We *"Trust in the Lord with our whole heart and lean not on our own understanding."* This policy has always proven to save us from decisions we might have made - ones that would have resulted in bad choices.

What I testify of now was something that happened many years ago. Our only daughter Susan was enrolled at The University of Georgia, working toward her master's degree. She was very involved with a group of young men and women known as Youth With a Mission (YWAM) who had planned a mission trip to Peru and then by boat up the Amazon River to minister to natives of that country who had never heard the good news of the Gospel.

She could not meet YWAM in California, where they planned to leave together as a group.

Consequently, she made arrangements to fly from the airport in Atlanta and meet them in Peru. Her flight would take her first to Germany, where she would board another flight from there to Peru.

This was during the days when the Berlin wall was still standing. She did not speak German but would be required to pass through areas with heavily armed German troops.

From the moment she left on her flight in Atlanta until the mission trip was completed and she returned home, we consistently prayed together, quoting the entirety of Psalm 91. Wherever Psalm 91 had the word 'you' or 'your,' we substituted *Susan*.

When the day came for Susan to return home to Atlanta, we went to greet her. It would be a late-night flight, so we were there earlier in the night and waiting down in the bottom of the airport where foreign flights unload and arriving passengers go through Customs. We waited for what seemed like forever but didn't see our daughter disembark and come through Customs.

Finally, we approached one of the airport's staff members and asked when her flight number would be landing. He responded: "Oh, that flight landed several hours ago."

Of course, my wife and I were deeply concerned and immediately made a phone call to the airlines on which Susan was traveling. The person we talked to was very nice, but after a few minutes of researching, she simply replied, "Susan McKinnon was a No Show for the flight out of London."

Can you possibly imagine the concern that welled up in our hearts when we heard that?

I suggested that we go back up the long stairs to the main area of the airport where the ticket counters were located. As we headed up those long staircases, we both began to pray loudly in the Spirit, not caring a bit about what others around us were thinking! As an afterthought, I later laughed that maybe people thought we were from some foreign country and praying aloud in our native language.

We finally reached the big area with all the airline registration and ticket booths. By now, it was very early morning; most of the lights had been turned off. There was only one airline that was still open, and that was the one our daughter had booked for her flight. The post was still open, but with just one station in service.

This one station had a long line of people waiting to be served, so we stood at the very end of that long line. We had been standing there only a few seconds when we heard a voice behind us saying: "You two seem to need some help."

As I turned around, I saw this tall, beautiful lady dressed in that airline's uniform. I replied, "Yes, we do!" She smiled and said, "Follow me."

She led us to the counter right next to the open one with the long line, took off her keys, opened the door, and turned on the lights and the computer in the booth. She then asked how she could help us. We told her our problem, and she said, "Let's see what I can find out."

She began skillfully working the computer, and in just a few seconds, she commented, "Ah, I find one S. McKinnon whose plane was delayed landing due to heavy air traffic and had to circle the airport until given permission to land. By the time that flight arrived, her scheduled flight from London to Atlanta had already departed." She continued searching.

"Let's see if we can trace where Susan McKinnon is now." In just a few seconds, she said, "Found her! She boarded another flight on a plane heading to a northern state in the U.S."

We must have looked bewildered because she added, "Don't worry. If we can get her in the U.S., we can absolutely get her home."

After just a second or two, she said, "I found her! She is on flight number so and so. Looking at her watch, she said, "This flight has already landed and should be unloading at the gate ...right now! She gave us the gate number and pointed the way. "If you hurry, you'll meet her there."

We turned around and took about three steps in the right direction when I realized I had not thanked her for such awesome help. We turned around to thank her, and the station was dark and closed with no one around it.

In awe, I said to my wife, "We have just been in the presence of an angel of the Lord." Praising God, we rushed to the place of disembarking, getting there just in time to see our daughter, Susan, coming through the door.

I share this testimony to say that I fully believe Jehovah-Shalom – the Lord my Peace and Jehovah-Jireh – The Lord that Sees and Supplies were working together that night long ago to protect and bless the three of us in a powerful and amazing way.

If you could have been with us that early morning as we were driving home with our daughter, you would have heard spontaneous praise and worship that entire trip! We had seen the God of Peace and the God of Provision very busy.

As the song we worship to often in our church says, "Our God is an Awesome God!"

5. Jehovah-Shammah means "the Lord is Present."

Today and every day, God is always present with us because – if we have been born again and are truly a son or daughter of God – we have His gift of the Holy Spirit with us.

Jesus clarifies this truth in John 14:15-17: *"If you love Me, keep My commandments, and I will pray to the Father, and He will give you another Helper* (Comforter), *that He may abide with you forever – The Spirit of truth, whom the world cannot receive, because it neither sees nor knows Him, but you know Him, for He dwells **with you** and **will be in you.**"*

Jesus was speaking of a time after His death on the cross and His resurrection from the grave. This event was also described in Acts 2:1-4.

Today, this is generally referred to as the Baptism of the Holy Spirit. I realize some churches don't believe this gift is possible in this day, but it's like my testimony stated earlier in this book: "You can't convince me there's no such thing as coffee because I taste it every day when I drink a cup."

So it is with the baptism of the Holy Spirit. He and I commune together many times every day. We are born again of the Holy Spirit, so we always have that spiritual connection with Him. Romans 8:16 records, *"The Spirit itself bears witness with our spirit, that we are the children of God"* (See also Romans 8:11, and 1 Peter 2:3).

6. Jehovah-Nissi means, "The Lord my Canopy."

Just like the shepherd uses the rod and staff to protect his sheep from wolves and other dangers, a canopy is a covering; it protects God's people.

Because we believe in God and are born again by the Spirit, He can and will protect us today as well. *"What shall we say to these things? If God be for us, who can be against us?"* (Romans 8:31)

The Prophet Isaiah, under the anointing of the Holy Spirit writes, *"No weapon formed against you shall prosper, and every tongue which rises against you in judgment you shall condemn. This is the heritage of the servants of the Lord, and their righteousness is from Me, says the Lord."*

The King James Version of Colossians 1:13 reads, *"...Who hath delivered us from the power of darkness, and hath translated (transported) us by the work of His dear Son."*

The Berean Study Bible translation, I believe more accurately, reads, *"He has rescued us from the dominion of darkness and brought us into the kingdom of His beloved Son."*

Many years ago, when I was just a small boy growing up on a farm, I spent a great deal of my time outdoors by myself. It wasn't because I didn't have other children to play with, but I guess I just loved to roam around by myself and see what I could discover.

Because of my adventurous spirit, I could share many experiences, which would exemplify the presence and work of Jehovah-Nissi protecting me. I chose these two childhood experiences because they reveal His presence and His canopy of protection very clearly.

The first event occurred when I was outside walking around and went to the barn in the back yard. My parents called me, and when I did not answer, they became concerned. They had seen me last as I was walking close to the barn, so that's where they started searching.

My Dad traced my footsteps where I had walked up to an old well inside the barn and stood looking over the edge. Other men in the neighborhood were helping by that time, and my Dad thought I had fallen into the well.

He found a long rope, put it around his waist, and told the guys to slowly lower him into the well. He felt sure I had drowned and wanted to retrieve my body.

Just as he was about to be lowered into the well, another neighbor who had walked out of the barn calling my name heard me respond from a cow pasture overgrown with weeds.

He quickly notified my parents and the others, and as they began the search, I walked up through the weeds to where they were. After questioning me, they found out I had indeed walked up and looked into the well but had decided to go "check on the cows." To this day, I am certain that day Jehovah-Nissi was "The Lord my Canopy!"

One other incident occurred when I had walked across the dirt road in front of our home and climbed up a big pecan tree. I climbed up fairly high to where a series of electrical lines ran through the tree. I remember how fascinating this was, so I broke off a small green limb from the tree and began drumming away on the electrical lines. After my power lines concert, I climbed down and went back to the house. I believe the only reason I was not electrocuted was that Jehovah-Nissi was there protecting me.

The last instance I'll describe came when I was a grown man with my wife and a family of four children. I have always loved the outdoors and especially loved fishing and hunting. One particular weekend, I had gone to the river with my friends to spend the whole weekend on the Ocmulgee River fishing limb lines and trotlines for catfish. We would rig the lines in the day and then check the lines each night and early each morning.

A good friend of mine and I were together in my boat checking a trotline we had placed in an area with a very strong current. Through a series of accidental events, my boat was capsized. The two of us were thrown into the water, neither of us wearing a life jacket floundering in the rapids.

I remember while I was underwater, the strong current was forcing me through the top of a huge tree which had fallen into the river. I felt like the limbs were surely going to beat me to death!

The next thing I knew, I was pushed into the back of the boat where the motor was mounted, and the propeller was still running. It seemed forever before I could get away from it. Finally, when I came up, I saw the capsized boat, swam to it, and got on top where my friend was waiting for me.

My only injury was a cut on my lower lip and my chin, which occurred during my battle with the propeller blade—rescued again by the presence and power of Jehovah-Nissi!

We must always keep in mind the various names of our heavenly Father and realize each of His names reveal His nature. As we come into alignment with His character and His will as recorded in the Holy Scriptures and are faithful to be obedient, we enter covenant with Him. We will talk about that covenant next.

The Father Figure in the Pattern of God's Eternal Spiritual Household

As previously stated, God our heavenly Father is the father of His eternal household. As we study the Scriptures, we must understand that, in addition to His other names and His nature, we find that God is a **God of Boundaries**.

This concept is clearly shown throughout the Scriptures; we begin to observe it in the creation of the heavens and the earth in Genesis 1.

As our heavenly Father, God has very specific requirements for those who desire to be a member of His family. These basic requirements can all be summed up by one word – "Obedience."

Our heavenly Father is a loving God but will not be moved by our ideas of what obedience means. He has outlined His requirements in a covenant carved in stone and known as the Ten Commandments. You can find it in Exodus 20:3-17. Take a moment and read those few verses.

As we live our lives in obedience to the requirements of His covenant, He is always quick to fulfill His part of the covenant. This enables us to become a member of His Eternal Household. As a result, we begin to grow in grace, knowledge, and understanding of God the Father, Jesus, God the Son, and God the Holy Spirit. We become more Christ-like in our daily lives. We begin to grow from a babe in Christ to a mature member of His household.

As we continue to abide in His household, we understand the simplicity of the kingdom of God. We become aware that *"the kingdom of God is not eating and drinking* (worldly life of the flesh) *but **righteousness, peace, and joy** in the Holy Spirit"* (Romans 14:17).

I daily measure myself by this standard. In other words, if during the day I find myself not in righteousness, peace, or joy, I realize I have stepped out of the boundary lines of the kingdom of God. I immediately confess my situation to God the Father, judge my actions as sin, repent from them, and ask God the Father through Jesus Christ to forgive me. I know He will forgive.

God's word says, *"The lord is not slack concerning His promise, as some count slackness, but is longsuffering toward us, not willing that any should perish but that all should come to repentance"* (2 Peter 3:9).

Furthermore, 1 John 1:9 assures us, *"If we confess our sins, He is faithful and just to forgive us our sins and to cleanse us from all unrighteousness."* What an awesome Father we have as members of His holy household.

The Holy Spirit – The Type and Shadow of a Godly Mother

This may be controversial, and it may not be what you've heard before, but hear me out. First, let me say clearly, I am not suggesting the Holy Spirit is a woman or effeminate or in any way inferior to God the Father or Jesus the Son. I do not believe that. This is an illustration, not a doctrine. With that in mind, let's examine one role of the Holy Spirit.

Just as God's pattern and plan for our earthly household requires a godly mother, so the pattern and plan for God's spiritual household also requires a godly mother. The Holy Spirit is a perfect example of a type and shadow of the godly mother in God's household.

This decision to believe the Holy Spirit is a type and shadow of a mother is based solely on the Word of God. As we examine some of the verses where Scripture provides insight into the nature and work of the Holy Spirit, keep this thought in mind: The female is the only member of the human population who can, through natural operations of life, become pregnant and produce offspring.

We easily accept this as truth not only in the human population but also in all species of the animal kingdom.

The Genesis account tells the History of Creation. The very first verse reads, *"In the beginning, God created the heavens and the earth. The earth was without form and void; and darkness was on the face of the deep. And the Spirit of God was hovering over the face of the waters. Then God said, 'Let there be light,' and there was light."*

This concept of "hovering over" reveals one of the awesome works of the Holy Spirit. In almost every recording of life and light being produced, we observe the hovering nature of the Holy Spirit.

In the Gospel of John, there is a dialogue recorded between Jesus Christ and a Pharisee named Nicodemus. Their conversation gives us more insight into the character type and shadow of the Holy Spirit.

This man came to visit Jesus by night and said, *"'Rabbi, we know that You are a teacher come from God; for no one can do these signs that You do unless God is with Him.' Jesus answered and said to him, 'Most assuredly, I say to you, unless one is born again, again,* (or, from above) *he cannot see the kingdom of God.' Nicodemus said to Him, 'How can a man be born when he is old? Can he enter a second time into his mother's womb and be born?' Jesus answered, 'Most assuredly, I say to you, unless one is born of the water* (referring to the natural birth process) *and the Spirit* (now referring to the new spiritual birth), *he cannot enter the kingdom of God. That which is born of the flesh is flesh, and that which is born of the Spirit is spirit"* (John 3:1-7).

As we continue to examine the Scriptures regarding this vital truth, we explore what we find written in 1 John 5:4-5, *"For whatever is born of God overcomes the world. And this is the victory that has overcome the world – our faith. Who is he who overcomes the world, but he who believes that Jesus is the Son of God?"*

We recognize we need to open our hearts to Jesus and invite Him to come into our hearts and become the Lord of our life. At that moment, the Holy Spirit - a type and shadow of the Mother in God's household - *delivers* another child of God.

We join God's family by supernatural birth. We become eligible for membership in His eternal household through the work of the Holy Spirit. It is a type or illustration of the natural birth being acted out by the Holy Spirit, producing a spiritual birth.

What an awesome change begins in the life of the newborn baby, as he or she begins to move from baby to mature son or daughter of the living God (See 2 Corinthians 5:17; 21).

Again, the Bible is our roadmap in our journey as we grow in Christ Jesus toward mature sons and daughters of God. The Scriptures again verify and confirm this eternal truth written in 1 John 5:4, *"For whatever is born of God overcomes the world. And this is the victory that has overcome the world – our faith."*

Only those who are born again by the Spirit can have faith! Hebrews 11:6 says, *"But without faith it is impossible to please Him* (God)*, For he who comes to God must believe that He is, and that He is a rewarder of those who diligently seek Him."*

Faith is defined very simply in the first verse of chapter Hebrews 11:*"Now faith is the substance* (realization) *of things hoped for, the evidence* (confidence) *of things not seen."*

Faith is not something we were born with in this natural life. Yet, we cannot be born again by the Spirit without faith. We read in Ephesians 2:8-9, *"For by grace you have been saved, and that not of yourselves; it is a gift of God, not of works, lest anyone should boast."*

Let's examine the word grace. There are several definitions of this word, but for this illustration, I prefer the one that defines grace as "The enabling power and ability of God."

The Holy Spirit, our type and shadow of the mother in God's Eternal Family, is also called "The Spirit of Grace." We know that God truly exists and the only way to abide in His household is to be born again by the Spirit. Knowing this, we understand the eternal truth - that we must be born again to spend eternity in heaven with Him, or we will spend eternity in Hell. It's just that simple.

Consequently, as we seek to know Jesus Christ as our personal Lord and Savior, the Holy Spirit provides two gifts of God - the gift of faith and the power of grace - both essential to being born again by the Spirit as a new creation.

The Apostle Paul proves this in his second letter to the Corinthians 5:17, *"Therefore, **if** anyone is in Christ, he is a **new creation**; old things have passed away; behold, all things have become new."* *If* is a conditional word in the passage. Without a decision to be *"in Christ,"* we cannot become a new creation. We must believe and accept God's offer to receive this new life (Romans 10:9,10).

Jesus Christ made this simple and powerful when He walked this earth as He was talking to His disciples and preparing them for His crucifixion. (See John 14:1-5).

Let me quote with emphasis verses five and six: *"Thomas said to Him, 'Lord, we do not know where You are going, and **how can we know the way?**' Jesus said to him, **I am the way**, the truth, and the life. **No one comes to the Father except through Me.**"* What does this mean?

Allow me to simplify what this really means and how essential it is that we understand this to become eligible to abide in God's household.

To become a new creature in Christ, we must be born again by recognizing God's simple yet powerful pattern and plan.

We must admit that without Jesus in our hearts, we are lost and without hope. We then must confess to the Lord that we have sinned, repent (turn away from our sins), ask Jesus to forgive our sins and cleanse us from all unrighteousness (Romans 3:23; 6:23; 5:8; 10:8,9).

Then we must open our hearts to Jesus and ask Him to be the **Lord** of our life. Revelation 3:20 records that the Lord says: *"Behold, I stand at the door* (of our heart) *and knock. If anyone hears My voice and **opens the door, I will come into Him and dine with him, and he with Me.**"* How simple and vital this eternal word of truth is; when we open the door, Jesus enters to become our Lord and Savior.

The sacrifice Jesus paid when He was crucified on the cross and poured out His life's blood was all a Holy God needed to purge our sins. Our carnal nature was banished into His sea of forgetfulness and remembered no more. You are now a child of God - albeit a baby - who now needs to grow up in the knowledge and obedience of God the Father.

Next, we will examine the role of Jesus Christ the Lord in God's Eternal Household. But before going any further, we need to understand the relationship of the Trinity – God the Father, God the Son, and God the Holy Spirit. Each has various roles and ministries, yet they are united as one.

In 1 Corinthians 12:4-7, Paul the Apostle, under the anointing of the Holy Spirit, writes, *"There are diversities of gifts, but the same Spirit. There are differences of ministries, but the same Lord. And there are diversities of activities, but <u>the</u>*

same God who works who works all in all." In other words, the Trinity is always in Unity!

Our God - who is love - has an awesome reward for those who live in unity. The Psalmist David writes these words in Psalm 133:1 and 3, *"Behold, how good and how pleasant it is for brethren to dwell together in unity* (verse 1) *"For there the Lord **commanded the blessing – life forevermore.***" (Verse 3b).

We see this unity of the Trinity when Jesus is baptized by John the Baptist in the Jordon River. As Jesus, the Son of God, came up from the water, the Holy Spirit appeared as a dove and lit upon Him, and the voice of God the Father spoke from heaven, saying, *'This is my beloved Son in whom I am well pleased."* (Matthew 3:16-17).

Jesus Christ – The Firstborn Son

The Apostle John records a verse most people have heard or read at some time in their lives. It's one thing to have read this portion of Scripture or even to believe it as truth. However, it's quite another thing to have had this verse become alive inside of you, to accept it in your heart, and to act upon it to become eligible for membership in God's eternal household.

John 3:16 reads, *"For God so loved the world that He gave His only begotten Son, that whoever believes in Him should not perish, but have everlasting life."*

Those who desire heaven as their eternal destiny when they die must receive Jesus Christ as the Lord of their life, obey His commands, grow in grace, and become obedient 'doers' of God's word.

This single act of belief is how we become a son or daughter, but the process of obedience is how we mature from a newborn son or daughter to a mature follower of God (James 1:22).

Those who do not believe, confess their sins, repent, and accept Jesus as their Lord and Savior are doomed to spend eternity in hell with Satan and his demons and all the others who are consigned to hell.

We must be aware of the truth that God is not willing that any should perish but that all should come to repentance (2 Peter 3:9). God has given all humanity the liberty to choose between serving Jesus and abiding in God's household eternally or choosing to serve Satan, the ruler of this world, and abiding in hell forever.

I implore those reading this book to choose Jesus Christ as your Savior and the Lord of your life and become God's child in His eternal household.

The eternal truth that Jesus is the firstborn of many sons and daughters of God is recorded many times in the Bible. (Matthew 1:25; Romans 8:29; Colossians 1:15,18; 1 Corinthians 15:23; and Revelation 1:5-6).

Oh, the greatness of God's goodness! During the Old Testament times, the firstborn son in a family was always given a double portion of the inheritance when the father died. Things greatly changed when Jesus came. It was a crucial part of His role as the Son in God's Household.

In the book of Acts, Saul had a life-changing encounter with the risen Lord Jesus. Saul, a Hebrew, was on his way to Damascus to persecute the Jews. He had been persecuting and killing the Jews of Nazareth and Jerusalem who accepted Jesus as their Messiah. On the road to Damascus, the risen Jesus appeared to Saul.

Jesus confronted Saul, whose name was later changed to Paul, saying *".... I will deliver you from the Jewish people, as well as from the Gentiles, to whom I now send you, to open their eyes, to turn them from darkness to light, and from the power of Satan to God, that they may receive forgiveness of sins, and an **inheritance** among those who are sanctified by faith in Me"*(Acts 26:12-18).

We must understand Jesus in light of the concept of a Jewish inheritance. We need to grasp what Jesus, the first-born, was entitled to receive. As we investigate this concept of *inheritance*, we find numerous Scriptures that shed light on the inheritance of God through Jesus Christ. They will help us understand how that includes all the children of God who abide in His household.

In Romans, we read, *"Therefore, brethren, we are debtors – not to the flesh, to live according to the flesh. For if you live according to the flesh, you will die, but if by the Spirit you put to death the deeds of the body, you will live. For as many as are led by the Spirit of God, these are the sons of God. For you did not receive the spirit of bondage again to fear, but you received the Spirit of adoption by whom we cry out 'Abba* (Father). *The Spirit Himself bears witness with our spirit that we are children of God, and if children, then heirs - heirs of God and* **joint-heirs with Christ***, if indeed we suffer with Him, that we may also be glorified together"* (Romans 8:12-17).

Even today, in the courts of this nation, an heir is anyone who inherits the assets of the deceased. A joint-heir is multiple people receiving some inheritance. In the case of our eternal heavenly household, we are all equal partners in the inheritance, joint-heirs with Christ.

Father God always confirms His word numerous times in the Bible. Ephesians 1:11 records, *'In Him* (Christ) *also we have obtained an inheritance, being predestined according to the purpose of Him who works all things according to the counsel of His will."*

In Colossians one, Paul compels us to give thanks to the Father who has qualified us. Paul says that those who have received Jesus as the Lord of their lives and been born again are partakers of the inheritance of the saints (verse 12).

Unlike heirs of an earthly inheritance, if we indeed qualify to abide forever in God's household, we have the opportunity to enjoy the benefits of that inheritance while on this earth. Jesus' death makes us heirs both now and in eternity!

In preparing His disciples for His departure, Jesus explains the role of the Holy Spirit. He said He would send the Holy Spirit to minister to them when He is raised from the dead and goes back to heaven to be with His Father.

"However, when He - the Spirit of truth, has come, He will guide you into all truth; for He will not speak on His own authority, but whatever He hears, He will speak; and He will tell you things to come. He will glorify Me, for He will take of what is Mine and declare it to you. ***All things that the Father has are Mine****. Therefore, I said He will take of Mine and declare it to you"* (John 16:13-15).

I wonder how many believing Christians grasp the powerful significance this revelation gives us about the inheritance we share as **joint-heirs** with Christ?

It's only through faith and by the Holy Spirit, the very Spirit of Grace, that we can comprehend what is *already* ours through faith to receive it in this life!

As stated previously, when we are born again, we are babes in Christ. As newborn babes in the natural realm, we must be fed the proper diet and given the appropriate care, so we can grow up and be healthy.

One of the saddest things I can think of is a baby that is not cared for properly. We grieve when we hear about children who are not given the proper care and die at a young age. The exact same thing very often happens in the spiritual realm.

As a minister, I have observed many fully mature grown adults who live their entire life as babes in Christ, never growing to maturity in the Spirit. In the natural, if we see a baby who is not able to walk or eat or function by a certain age, we know something is not normal. The same is true in the Spirit. God intends us to grow in faith.

The writer of Hebrews addresses this truth that was also a problem in those days. *"For though by this time you ought to be teachers, you need someone to teach you again the first principles of the oracles of God; and you need milk and not solid food. For everyone who partakes only of milk is unskilled in the word of righteousness, for he is a babe. But solid food belongs to those who are of full* (or mature) *age, that is, those who* **by reason of use** *have their senses* **exercised by** *practice to discern* **both good and evil.**"

Very simply, we must know the word of God by reading, daily study, and putting what we have learned about the will, the ways, and the commandments of God into daily practice.

Back in my early high school days, I needed to lasso cattle from horseback to treat them for parasites and keep them in good health. A friend of mine was quite good at this skill, but I was struggling. He told me that if I wanted to improve, I had to practice while standing on the ground before I even tried to rope a calf from horseback.

He set a bale of hay in front of me, long side forward, and standing ten feet behind the bale, lassoed the very front end of the bale. My goal was to successfully rope this hay bale one hundred times in a row before even trying to catch a calf from horseback.

You cannot possibly imagine how many hours I practiced before I was skilled enough to complete the assignment.

I spent many hours roping hay bales before I was ready to even try roping running calves from a moving horse. That practice helped me develop into an experienced and successful rodeo calf roper. I successfully performed my responsibilities on the farm and won a good deal of money calf roping in rodeos. I went through the hours and hours of practice because it was a desire of my heart to become proficient at this skill.

The same is true in the realm of the Spirit. We must have the desire to grow up as mature children of God by applying the gifts He has given us, then help other babes in Christ do the same.

Spiritual growth should be an inherent part of the life of one who is truly born again. God has freely given each of us newborn babes in Christ all we need to grow and mature in the Spirit. He has provided us with the gift of faith, the gift of the Holy Spirit, also known as the Spirit of Grace or the enabling power and ability of God Himself.

God redeemed us through the sacrifice of His only begotten Son and imputed Jesus Christ's righteousness to us.

He has also given us His Holy Word to guide us in our growth process. We grow by being obedient to His commandments. It's our choice to be *"Doers of the Word, and not hearers only, deceiving yourselves"* (James 1:22).

The Word of God is packed with powerful truths but presented with simplicity. To be eligible to abide in His household, we must grow in grace spiritually and simply do what He says and what He directs us through His word to do.

The Apostle James states bluntly that faith without works is dead. God did not give us dead faith (James 2:14-20). The word *"works"* is also referred to as *"fruit"* in many other places, and Jesus Christ used these words when describing how important our works are for us to be residents in God's household. John recorded the parable of the True Vine.

We will examine a few portions of Scripture that are crucial for our understanding here, but I urge readers to review the entire selection independently. Remember, God is a God of love, but He is also a God of wrath, and this revelation should prompt in us a healthy and holy fear of the Lord.

Jesus begins this parable by saying, *I am the true vine, and My Father is the vinedresser.* **Every branch in Me that does not bear fruit He takes away."** (Verse 2).

In verse 6, we read, *"If anyone does not abide in Me,* **he is cast out as a branch and is withered;** *and they gather them and* **throw them into the fire, and they are burned."** This clearly indicates one who is in His household can be cast out and no longer qualified to be an active member in His household.

I am deeply grieved to observe so many who claim to be Christians, yet, by choosing not to be obedient, fail to fulfill the purpose and plan of God for their life here on earth. We are all created to be destined for eternity, yet we often take so much for granted that we fail to realize the eternal truth that eternity is only one heartbeat away.

The Word of God states, *"It is appointed for men to die once, but after this the judgment"* (Hebrews 9:27).

This eternal truth is confirmed by Paul when he writes, *"For we must all appear before the judgment seat of Christ, that each one may receive the things done in the body, according to what he has done, whether good or bad. Knowing, therefore, the terror of the Lord, we persuade men; but we are well known to God, and I also trust, are well known in your consciousness"* (2 Corinthians 5:10-11).

As we close this section of the book, we must realize that God's Word details a list of lifestyles that are totally forbidden to be a part of His eternal household. I listed only one portion of Scripture here, but assure you other portions refer to the same type of people on the earth today.

This list is from Paul's letter to the Galatians, where he lists the works of the flesh as compared to the works of the Spirit.

Paul writes, *"Now the works of the flesh are evident, which are adultery, fornication, uncleanness, lewdness, sorcery, hatred, contentions, idolatry, outbursts of wrath, selfish ambitions, dissensions, heresies, envy, murder, drunkenness, reveries, and the like; of which I tell you beforehand, just as I also told you in time past, that* **those who practice such things will not inherit the kingdom of God**" (Galatians 5:19-21).

This is a specific list of lifestyles, but we need to be aware God is a Holy God, and as we have stated earlier, without holiness, no one will see God. This seems hopeless until we realize He has given us all we need to lead a holy life while we're on this earth.

These lifestyles are further described in the Old Testament in a list of seven things that God calls an "abomination" in His sight.

King Solomon, the most intelligent man to ever live on the earth, wrote in Proverbs 6:16-19, *"These six things the Lord hates, yes, seven are an abomination to Him: A proud look* (See James 4:6),

A lying tongue, Hands that shed innocent blood, (We will review the abortion statistics later point in this book) *A heart that devises wicked plans, Feet that are swift in running to evil, A false witness who speaks lies, And one who* **sows discord among the brethren***."*

These are all people who cannot possibly inherit or abide in the eternal Household of God unless they believe in the sacrifice of the only begotten Son of God, Jesus Christ. They must repent for their sins, and accept and honor Jesus Christ as the Lord of their life to be born again by the Spirit of God.

To be a member of God's eternal spiritual household requires an eternal spiritual choice. Only by making a decision to join God's family can we become part of His eternal spiritual household.

The Pattern of the Church God's Spiritual Household on Earth

Just as we have studied the household of God and the earthly household of a family, God also has a **pattern** (plan, design, or order) for the Church, the Body of Christ on Earth.

In many ways, it follows His pattern for a godly earthly household and a godly eternal household. There are many different churches of various denominations, types, styles, and designs. However, many of them are not built following what I believe to be God's design in the Holy Scriptures.

I write this not to express judgment but to suggest the Scriptures be thoroughly studied when it comes to this subject. I will submit what I believe with all my heart is the will, way, and design for God's Church on the earth. It's up to others to apply it in their church family.

I am convinced and convicted that each of the three households I present in this book is designed to operate according to His pattern and plan. It is absolutely essential that every structure must be built on a strong, healthy foundation. Otherwise, it will eventually collapse.

I confess that I am, of all things, not a very effective carpenter. I know little about the proper construction of buildings of any type. Because I have not been in construction, I have very little comprehension of the appropriate way to create a foundation for a large structure. However, I have a

Christian brother who is well qualified to construct a solid foundation. He has helped me tremendously, explaining the basics of building a solid structure on a stable foundation.

The first principle is, the foundation determines the strength of the entire structure.

It requires the most work and planning because it determines the integrity of the entire building. I am told that much time and labor are needed to dig where the building will be located to find a strong and sturdy place to support the finished structure.

There is more time and work involved in establishing the foundation than any other time in completing the construction.

Once the foundation is dug and poured, the first step in any strong building, natural or spiritual, is the first stone put in place – the cornerstone.

All the other building stones must be placed in order, so they line up with the cornerstone. This is the only way for the building to be solid, safe, and enduring. Everything rests on the cornerstone.

We observe this absolute, eternal truth in several places in the Word of God. We begin our search by going back to the days of Abraham, who is also called "The Father of Faith."

Hebrews 11:8-10 states, *"By faith, Abraham obeyed when he was called to go out to the place which he would receive as an inheritance. And he went out, not knowing where he was going. By faith, he dwelt in the land of promise as in a foreign country, dwelling in tents with Isaac and Jacob the heirs with him of the same promise; for he waited for the city* **which has foundations whose builder and maker is God.**"

Jesus Christ Himself is the builder of the Church! Jesus makes this absolutely clear in a conversation with His disciples when He asks them a very pertinent question recorded in Matthew's gospel, chapter 16 verses 13-19.

The Lord begins with the question, *Who do men say that I, the Son of man, am? So they said, 'Some say John the Baptist, some Elijah, and others Jeremiah or one of the prophets.' He said to them, but who do you say that I am?"*

I pause here to say that this is the most important question of all eternity. At some time, every person who has ever dwelt on this earth must answer that question for themselves. Each one's answer determines where they will spend eternity - in heaven with God the Father and Jesus the Lord, or in Hell! The discussion continues,

"Simon Peter answered and said, 'You are the Christ the Son of the living God.' Jesus answered and said to him, blessed are you, Simon Bar-Jonah, for flesh and blood has not revealed this to you, but My Father who is in heaven. And I also say to you that you are Peter, and on this rock (literally, this rock of revelation) I will build My church, and the gates of Hades shall not prevail against it. And I will give you the keys of the kingdom of heaven, and whatever you bind on earth will be bound in heaven, and whatever you loose on earth will be loosed in heaven."

I take the liberty of repeating here Paul's revelation in Ephesians 2:19-22, *"Now, therefore, you are no longer strangers and foreigners, but fellow citizens with the saints and members of the household of God, having been built on the foundation of the apostles and prophets,* **Jesus Christ Himself being the <u>chief cornerstone</u>**, *in* *whom the whole building, being fitted together, grows into a holy temple in the Lord, you also are being built together for a dwelling place of God in the Spirit."*

It is imperative that those reading this book understand most clearly that these verses refer only to those who have opened their hearts to Jesus Christ, confessed their sins, repented from them, and received Him both as the Lord of their life and as their personal Savior.

Only after this decision will they become born again by the Spirit and become a new creation in Christ. We must further realize that we are spiritual newborn members of His household. We are required to grow in the Spirit.

Through this growing process, we become *"doers of the word and not hearers only, deceiving ourselves"* (James 1:22). Being a doer of the word simply means to study the Holy Scriptures and do what the written Word of God says.

We must also realize that God's grace is the enabling ability and power of God through the Holy Spirit, also called "The Spirit of Grace," and who lives inside us. We must also be aware of what the word of God tells us, *"God resists the proud, but gives grace to the humble"* (James 4:6).

Let's continue with our earlier illustration of foundations and buildings and cornerstones. In the household of God, we understand that Jesus Christ is THE Cornerstone.

That design, that Foundation, helps us fully understand how those other foundation stones must be set. Every stone is laid in relation to and lined up with that first stone, the Cornerstone.

In our building, we will also find six other stones in the formation of the Church on earth today. Combined with Christ, the Cornerstone, these six stones give us seven stones in the earthly household of God. We call this building, this household, the Church.

Consequently, our understanding of those other six stones in the foundation is essential to get the full picture of the construction of the foundation and what our responsibilities are in the building process. Furthermore, we must also realize the vital importance of a solid foundation Jesus spoke of in the Scriptures and the dire warning He makes concerning a poor foundation (See Matthew 7:24-25 and Luke 6: 46-49).

Many years ago, even before I was called into the ministry as a pastor, I was out in a pecan orchard early one morning reading in the book of Proverbs, which I fondly call "the wisdom of God." I came across this verse in Chapter 9, verse 1.

The verse seemed to jump off the page. It reads, *"Wisdom has built her house, She has hewn out her seven pillars..."* I immediately thought of the church and remembered that Jesus is the cornerstone and asked the Holy Spirit for a greater understanding of how this fit into the household of God.

The Church was built on the foundation of the apostles and prophets, with Jesus being the Chief Cornerstone. I am so glad that in Luke 11:9-10 Jesus said, *"So I say to you, ask, and it will be given to you; seek and you will find; knock, and it will be opened to you. For everyone who asks receives, and he who seeks finds, and to him who knocks it will be opened."*

Immediately after asking the Holy Spirit for a greater understanding, He directed me to the 5th and 6th chapters of Hebrews.

In chapter 5:12 through chapter 6:2, we find direction for those who were supposed to be members of the faith: *"For though by this time you ought to be teachers, you still need someone to teach you again the first principles of the oracles* (sayings or Scriptures) *of God; and you have come to need milk and not solid food. For everyone who partakes only of milk is **unskilled** in the **word of righteousness**, for he is a **babe**. For solid food belongs to those who are full of age* (mature), *that is, those who by **reason of use*** (practice) *have their senses exercised to discern both good and evil."*

Now we move to the sixth chapter to discover the listing of what I believe to be the other six foundation stones. I have listed them in the order as they accompany the cornerstone and complete the seven pillars cited in the passage quoted earlier from Proverbs.

We pick up where we left off and begin reading in the first verse of chapter 6. In verse 1, the writer continues, *"Therefore, leaving the discussion of the elementary principles of Christ, let us go on to perfection* (maturity), *not laying again the **foundation** of*

(1) *repentance from dead works, and of*
(2) *faith toward God,*
(3) *of the doctrine of baptisms,*
(4) *of laying on of hands,*
(5) *of* the *resurrection of the dead, and*
(6) *of eternal judgment."*

Let's examine the pattern of the authorities established by Jesus Christ for the church to function as He designed it to influence, impact, and change society today.

Again, as we examine the original pattern God has laid out for the building and ruling of the church, we can easily see the tactics of Satan. In this day and time, the current church bears practically no resemblance to the pattern of the original church.

Many (if not most) of our churches in America look nothing like the church Jesus and His disciples established in the first century.

To uncover the original biblical pattern for the church, we need only go back in history to the founding of this great nation.

I cannot for the life of me believe that God did not have His hand at work in a powerful and anointed way through the founding fathers of this great nation!

There was simply no way for them to be able to look forward so far into the future to see what kind of lifestyle we would be living today, and yet that's precisely what they have done in drawing up the legal blueprint of how this nation was designed to be structured! They gave us a great foundation.

A brief study of American history reveals that when the first pilgrims began the journey to establish colonies in this new land, they brought godly ministers. I highly recommend the book written years ago entitled, *The Light and the Glory.*

Eventually, every colony had at least one minister, known more commonly in those days as "The Man of God." His purpose in each settlement was to teach them the will and ways of Almighty God, their heavenly Father.

When unforeseen problems arose and the colony members didn't know what to do, the "Man of God" would call for a time of fasting and prayer to seek the Lord about what He wanted them to do.

According to verifiable accounts of these early days in the new land, when such a decree was given, every man, woman, and child ceased all activity and obeyed what "The Man of God" had ordered. Usually, it didn't take very long in fasting and prayer before God began to reveal His answer to the "Men of God," who would announce it to the colonists. When they followed the directions of the "Men of God," they would usually see positive results almost immediately.

Many interesting accounts are documented in this book that detail accounts of the first nation peoples who were in this new land. Where they were once in conflict with the pilgrims, they were soon converted to Christianity and became friends and protectors of the pilgrims.

Allow your mind to wander with me as we imagine life in those early colonial days. Citizens of England became disgruntled over the abusive taxation without representation rulings of the government. The abuse stirred many citizens to consider searching for a place to establish their new homes and form a new and unique form of human government.

Word had already begun to spread about the first group of men and their families who had loaded all their worldly goods aboard a sailing vessel and launched out to discover such a place. Based on these reports, new shiploads of people set sail to establish new lives for themselves and their families in this new land.

Consequently, new colonies of people began to spring up on the shores of this new continent. As these new colonists arrived, they were largely unaware of eyes watching from the heavy trees and bushes of the new land. Nor could they see these eyes were from a people who had a different skin color than they had.

These red-skinned people, later misnamed 'Indians,' were not happy to have white-skinned strangers occupying their land. Many battles occurred between the two groups, but both groups enjoyed planting and harvesting a very important crop for people and an essential food for their livestock–corn. It would eventually become both a life-sustaining resource and a bartering staple.

An adequate water supply was essential for growing a good corn crop, and both Indians and the new colonists depended heavily on good rains during the tasseling season. That is the time when the corn tassels bloom and produce pollen. This process is crucial for the corn to be fertilized and enables it to grow an abundant crop.

During one season, there was little rainfall, so the Men of God called for a time of fasting and prayer to seek God for rains. God honored these times of prayers and fasting, and gentle rainfalls began to come.

Although the colonists were unaware of it, the Indians watched very carefully what these new people did. They observed these times when the rains came upon the colonists, but either did not fall on their corn crop or, if it did, it was a hard, heavy rain that knocked much of their corn crop to the ground, rendering it un-harvestable.

A strange thing began to take place between the Indian natives and colonists. The Indians began to approach the colonists carefully, and both the Indians and colonists began to learn the other's language.

With their new-found communication, the Indians asked the colonist why their corn crops received gentle and productive rainfall when the rains they needed were either non-existent or fell so hard it knocked the corn down, causing poor yields.

These conversations opened the door for the colonists to share their faith in a living God who loved them and gave His only Son Jesus Christ to die on their behalf so they could give their lives to Him as their Lord and not perish but have everlasting life.

Many Indians soon accepted this Gospel, and it began to spread widely across this newly forming nation. What an awesome story and all of it recorded based on verifiable research data recovered over the years.

It doesn't take a rocket scientist to see how subtle Satan can be when he decided it's to his benefit to cover over a plan or pattern of God.

The further away from God's pattern and plan Satan can convince mankind to drift, the more corruption enters the scene. Corruption causes confusion and every evil work.

Under these circumstances, slowly but surely, an organization will drift like an unanchored and uncharted vessel. While I do not refer to all (or perhaps even most) of the churches in this great nation of America that we live in, it has certainly and subtly had a most negative effect on the way our society lives.

It all has taken place as the result of building our nation on a poor foundation. God designs the church in a country to stand and thrive through the pattern outlined in the Holy Scriptures.

We cover the pattern of the church in other portions of this book. However, we must understand certain absolute truths and requirements we must adhere to for the Church to operate according to the plan, the will, and way of God the Father and Jesus

Christ the Lord. Consequently, we go back to the Word and the Spirit.

In Paul's letter to the Ephesians, he compares marriage to Christ and the church. In Ephesians 5:25-27, he says, *"Husbands, love your wives, just as Christ also loved the church and gave Himself for her, that He might sanctify and cleanse her with the washing of water by the word, that He might present her to Himself a glorious church, not having spot or wrinkle or any such thing, but she should be holy and without blemish."*

As I consider these words, I often see churches that appear less like a vibrant living fruit and more like an old, wrinkled prune. They look nothing like the organization and structure clearly outlined in the Holy Scriptures. That is from my perspective as well as research data which we will discuss later in this book.

Jesus Christ is the builder of the Church (Matthew 16:18). I have often heard ministers refer to "my church," meaning, of course, the church they pastor. I simply hold my tongue instead of saying, "No, it is not! The church belongs to Jesus and not any human being!"

There are many churches and denominations throughout this nation, and most of them have their own **plan** and **pattern** for how their church is organized and how they function.

I will not attempt to outline a specific organizational structure here as many are effective. I will, however, describe the structure and organizational pattern we believe the Lord has given us to follow in the church I have been a part of from the first step to the current state. This is the same church I have been a part of since it was planted by a godly friend in the Spring of 1987.

The deeper I dig in the word of God, the more I realize this is true. God Himself was speaking through the Holy Spirit to godly men of old who, under the power and direction of the Holy Spirit, penned the plan and purpose of a loving God to His people. People wanted to see *"His kingdom come and His will done on earth as it is in heaven."*

We mentioned earlier that Paul compares the relationship of the church to the relationship between a husband and wife.

I remember hearing a respectful minister once say that he does not see a perfect, spotless, beautiful bride when he sees many churches across the nation. Instead, he said he sees a wrinkled, spotted, and blemished organization trying to function as a church of Jesus Christ. I have seen some churches which bear no resemblance to the church Paul describes, and it's sad.

I honestly am not trying to be judgmental, but often I observe the practice of having the entire church membership vote to elect or reject a new pastor they are considering. Yet, I know many of those voting members do not study the Word of God nor have an intimate relationship with the Holy Spirit. How well can they be expected to hear from God and vote accordingly?

I say this because of an incident I had years ago with a young man who was an elder in this local church. We discussed this openly, but no change was made in the years that followed.

Let's go back to the Word and the Spirit and see what the **pattern** and the **plan** of God are regarding this matter. Consider again the writings of Paul to the Ephesus, beginning in chapter 4 verse 7. Paul starts with his revelation on Spiritual Gifts.

As we read this portion of Scripture, we can see that Paul is referring to Jesus Christ. Notice verse 11 where Paul says, *"And He Himself (Jesus) gave some to be apostles, some prophets, some evangelists, and some pastors and teachers."*

These ministry gifts Jesus gave to the church are generally referred to as "The Five-fold Ministry Gifts." The purpose of these five-fold ministry gifts is outlined in verses 12-16:

*"...for the equipping of the saints for the work of ministry, for the edifying of the body of Christ till we all come to the unity of the faith, and of the knowledge of the Son of God, to a perfect man, to the measure of the stature of the fullness of Christ; that we should no longer be children, tossed to and fro and carried about with every wind of doctrine, by the trickery of men, in the cunning craftiness of deceitful plotting, but speaking the truth in love, may **grow up** in all things into Him who is the head - Christ - from whom the whole body, joined and knit together **by what every joint supplies, according to the effective working by which every part does its share, causes growth of the body for the edifying of itself in love.**"*

This portion of Scripture is the **pattern** of God for the flesh and bone body parts of Jesus Christ.

Notice that according to the Bible, this pattern involves the ministry of the entire five-fold ministry discussed earlier. For the purpose and plan of God to be effective, all the gifts should operate effectively in the church.

This does not mean that all the five-fold ministers must be on staff at any church. However, I believe they should be involved—some as staff and others as guest ministers who visit or preach throughout the year.

In many churches scattered over America, the membership expects the Senior Pastor to do all the preaching, visit the sick, and counsel those who need advice. The pastor is also expected to win the lost to Jesus and bring them into the local assembly.

Oh, how far we have strayed off course. I have a favorite saying: "Shepherds don't beget sheep – sheep beget sheep."

I'll never forget the time many years ago. I had no idea the Lord would call me to be a pastor at that time, but I was witnessing to people wherever I went and leading many to salvation.

One day, I was in my County Agent's office when the janitor (who also pastored a local assembly) came into my office with a young man and said to me, "I'd like for you to meet this young man who has some problems he's dealing with."

I welcomed the young man and began to ask him what was going on in his life. As he shared the struggles he was having; the part-time janitor pastor stood in the doorway listening.

After hearing his story, I explained to the young man that he was living in sin, which was why he was struggling. Then I began to share with the young man who Jesus was and the sacrifice He had made so that we could be saved through Him and have a real-life relationship with a Holy God – his heavenly father and his creator.

The young man was intrigued by what I told him, so I simply asked him if he would like to give his life to Jesus Christ, our Lord and Savior, and live his life for Him. Oh, was he ready! I led him through a sinner's prayer, and he committed his life to the lordship of Jesus. I rejoiced with him, and as they left my office, the janitor/pastor said, "I knew you would know what to do with him."

Although I rejoiced at that day, I fear some church members today are like that part-time pastor and janitor. They see the need and bring the person to a pastor rather than meeting the need themselves.

I have seen this same concept in the church where I served as Senior Pastor for many years. The word of God says: *"The righteous are bold as a lion."* Oh, that the church members in this current age would begin to fulfill their part of the word of God in Ephesians – being the Body of Christ.

We must emphasize that God reveals His purpose and His calling for all who are born again members of the flesh and bone body of Christ Jesus. He has made provisions and given direct orders for how we are designed to fulfill His calling to each one of us. We have a mission and a warning.

"For we all appear before the judgment seat of Christ, that each one may receive the things done in the body, according to what he has done, whether good or bad. Knowing, therefore, the terror of the Lord, we persuade men; but we are well known to God, and I also trust we are well known in your consciences" For the love of Christ compels us, because we judge thus; that if One died for all, then all died; and He died for all, that those who live should live no longer for themselves, but for Him who died for them and rose again" (2 Corinthians 5:10-15).

Let's consider what Paul writes in verses 18-20: *"Now all things are of God, who has reconciled us to Himself through Jesus Christ, and has given to us the ministry of reconciliation, that God was in Christ reconciling the world to Himself, not imputing (reckoning) their trespasses to them, and has committed to us the word of reconciliation. Now then, we are ambassadors for Christ, as though God were pleading through us; we implore you on Christ's behalf, be reconciled to God."*

There is an old hymn that we used to sing in the traditional churches where I was raised, and it comes flooding back to my mind when I observe the church. The chorus goes,

"Rise up oh men of God,
Be done with lesser things.
Give heart and soul, and mind and strength,
To serve the King of Kings."

In congregations over this nation, it's high time that we rise up and fulfill our calling and responsibilities. It's time for those who profess to be born again Christians to lay aside the "babe in Christ" mindset and grow up and take our place in the kingdom of God!

According to the word of God, all churches are commanded to have elders who are actively involved in the growth and ministry of their local assembly. The book of Acts records the disciples *"...appointed elders in every church"* (Acts 14:23).

In his letter to Titus, Paul outlines God's **pattern** for selecting elders: *"For this reason, I left you in Crete, that you should set in order the things that are lacking, and appoint elders in every city as I commanded you – If a man is blameless, the husband of one wife, having faithful children not accused of dissipation."*

Some translations read, *'debauchery.'* It literally means to be incorrigible or insubordinate.

Paul continues, *"For a bishop* (literally, overseer) *must be blameless, as a steward of God, not self-willed, not quick-tempered, not given to wine, not violent, not greedy for money, but hospitable, a lover of what is good, sober-minded, just, holy, self-controlled, holding fast to the faithful word as he has been taught, that he may be able, by sound doctrine, both to exhort and convict those who contradict"* (Titus 1:7).

Elders appointed by the Senior Pastor should be united in supporting the Pastor and the local assembly members. When there is unity among the Pastor, the Elders, and the members of the local assembly, the church will realize great power.

Considerer the word of God penned by David: *"Behold, how good and how pleasant it is for brethren to dwell together in **unity**! It is like the precious oil upon the head, running down on the beard, the beard of Aaron, running down the edge of his garments. It is like the dew of Hermon, descending upon the mountains of Zion; **For there (unity)** the Lord **commanded** the blessing-life forevermore"* (Psalm 133:1-3).

When the body, the church, functions as it should, there is unity, efficiency, and balance. On the other hand, where confusion exists, the results are vastly different.

Acts 19:32 reads: *"Some, therefore, cried one thing and some another, for the assembly was confused, and most of them did not know why they had come together."*

Paul continues to Titus: *"Reject a divisive man after the first and second admonition, knowing that such a person is warped and sinning, being self-condemned"* (Titus 3:10).

A divisive person can wreak havoc in a local assembly and desperately needs to be confronted by the Senior Pastor and the elders. Overlooking such a person can lead to confusion for the entire assembly. If left unaddressed, dissention could result in a church split.

God's order, His pattern, is essential for the church to function fully and godly.

The Pattern of the Earthly Family Household

As we examined the pattern of the earthly family's household, we must realize that God has ordained that it be built and managed according to how His eternal household is composed and managed.

The father of the earthly family's household should be very similar to God's pattern in His eternal household, the Church.

Consequently, let's examine some of the traits of the father in the earthly household. The father's role is paramount if this household is to be healthy, prosperous, and a candidate to receive the blessings of God.

I was blessed to be born into a family that fulfilled these requirements. Allow me to describe the nature and lifestyle of my earthly father, whom I called "Daddy" or "Dad."

He and my mother were the parents of four children - three boys and one girl. My oldest brother was the firstborn, and I was next. My sister and younger brother followed.

During my early years, my Daddy's only sibling - his sister - was married and had two children, both small boys. Her husband was a great man, but he died young, leaving Dad's sister to raise the two boys. Around a year later, Dad's sister became very sick. On her deathbed, she asked my Dad to adopt her two children and raise them on her behalf.

Dad did adopt those children and raise them as his own. Although my sister and younger brother have passed away, I still consider these two men Dad adopted as brothers in my heart.

As I grew older, I began to learn some things about my natural Dad. He graduated from a business school and desired to enter the business field as his vocation. However, his own father, who owned a large farm and ran a large store in a rural community, became sick and could not manage the farm and the country store. My Dad took over the operation of the farm and the business, laying aside his true desire to enter the business world as he yearned to do.

His business background, however, aided him in making both the farm and the country store a success. He consistently bought other farms that were for sale and either added these acres to his own farm or sold them to others for a nice profit.

Until his early death at age seventy-five, he demonstrated the life of a godly husband and father throughout his life. Using my Dad as our example, we will examine the pattern, plan, and requirements revealed in the Scriptures for an earthly father.

First, the father of the earthly family must be a godly man himself. Evidence of this trait is shown in a lifestyle that lines up with the word of God. One of the God-given responsibilities of the earthly father's household is to teach the household's children by word and lifestyle. He should *live* the nature, plan, and purposes of the eternal heavenly Father, not merely speak about it.

The prophet Ezekiel, writes:" *The living, only the living **man**, shall praise You, as I do this day; the **father** shall make known Your truth to the children"* (Isaiah 38:19).

Joel, 1 verse 3 is again written and directed to fathers: *"Tell your children about it (the mighty works of God), let your children tell their children, and their children, and their children another generation."*

God is often very specific with His commandments for godly fathers. Many of those commandments are followed by a promise. Such is the case recorded by Moses in Deuteronomy 11, where he addresses fathers and their responsibilities to their earthly families.

"You shall teach them (the ways of God) *to your children, speaking of them when you sit in your house, when you walk by the way, when you lie down, and when you rise up. And you shall write them on the doorposts of your house and on your gates."*

Notice God's promise to those who follow His commandment:*"...your days and **the days of your children may be multiplied in the land which the Lord swore to your fathers to give them, like the days of the heavens above the earth**"* (Deuteronomy 11:19-21).

For further references to this commandment, see Psalm 78:2-7, Deuteronomy 4:9, and 6:7. My earthly father did not spend much time with us reading the Scriptures and teaching us these things in scheduled sessions. However, he lived a life that was directed by these very principles.

He would absolutely be sure all of us never missed a Sunday when we would go to church together as a family, and he would often teach during the Sunday morning's Sunday School to the members of the little country church where we were members.

His lifestyle was a constant and consistent testimony of the will and ways of God the heavenly Father. I was greatly blessed to have a godly father who provided godly counsel for his children. I was also blessed to have a godly mother - one who guided all her children by daily teaching us the will and the ways of God.

I'll be covering this aspect of the plans and patterns of God, which require a godly mother in His household as well as in the earthly family's household. However, at this point, I owe it to my readers to share the journey I was led on by the Holy Spirit. It brought me the amazing revelation that confirmed the ways and the plan of God for a healthy household – both spiritually and naturally.

My journey began in the latter part of 1984 as I was sitting on a deer stand before daylight. In those pre-dawn times, I was communing with the Lord and asking Him why I was so blessed. He answered my question by saying, *"For everyone to whom much is given, from him much will be required; and of whom much has been committed, of him, they will ask the more"* (Luke 12: 48b).

I realized the Lord would expect more from me than I realized but had no concept whatever that He would later call me into the ministry as a Pastor.

Fast forward two years. I was seated at my desk in my church office. It was a hot summer day, and I decided to drive to a nearby convenience store to purchase a soft drink. As I drove into the parking lot and was about to get out, I heard a very loud sound of what I called "Junk Music" coming from a car heading to the same store.

The windows were down, and the radio was turned up so loud anyone for blocks away could hear it. The car was one of the fanciest and most expensive I had ever seen - one that when the driver stopped the center of the wheels kept spinning.

The driver who stepped out was a young guy who had to hold up his pants at the crotch to keep them from falling off. Even then, far too much was revealed!

I could feel a wave of deep anger rising in me. I wanted to confront the young man and chastise him. That's when the Holy Spirit spoke to me and said, "You know nothing about that young man! You don't even know if he knows who his father is!"

It was indeed a sharp word from the Holy Spirit. I was suddenly filled with compassion for the young man. I confessed the sin of judgementalism and asked God for forgiveness.

God's word says, *"If we confess our sins, He is faithful and just to forgive us our sins and to cleanse us from all unrighteousness"* (1 John 1:9).

This young man may be one of many who have no fatherly influence in his life. During my tenure as a Pastor, I have counseled several young men in the same situation. Often, they would begin to weep, and many would literally cry out in a loud voice saying: "I didn't even know my daddy's name until I was in my mid-twenties!"

Herein lies a tremendous problem all across America. Let's examine some shocking statistics concerning Fatherless Homes:
- 63% of youth suicides are from fatherless homes - five times the national average. (US Dept. of Health/Census)
- 90% of all homeless and runaway children are from fatherless homes - thirty-two times the average.

- 85% of all children who show behavior disorders come from fatherless homes - twenty times the average. (Center for Disease Control).
- 80% of rapists with anger problems come from fatherless homes - 14 times the average. (Justice & Behavior, Vol 14, p. 403-26).
- 71% of all high school dropouts come from fatherless homes - nine times the national average. (National Principals Association Report).
- **Father Factor in Education:** Fatherless children are twice as likely to drop out of school. Children with Fathers who are involved are more likely to get A's in school. Children with Fathers who are involved are more likely to enjoy school and engage in extracurricular activities.
- 75% of all adolescent patients in chemical abuse centers come from fatherless homes - ten times the average.
- **Father Factor in Drug and Alcohol Abuse:** Researchers at Columbia University found that children living in two-parent households with a poor relationship with their father are 68% more likely to smoke, drink, or use drugs than all teens in two-parent households. Teens in a single-mother household are at a 30% higher risk in those areas than those in two-parent households.
- 70% of youths in state-operated correction institutions grew up in homes with no father - 20 times the average. (Fulton County Georgia, Texas Dept. of Correction).
- Adolescent girls raised in a two-parent home with active dads are significantly less likely to

be sexually active than girls raised without dads in their lives.
- 71% of pregnant teenagers lack a father. (U.S. Department of Health and Human Services press release).
- **Father Factor in Incarceration:** Even after controlling for income, youths in father-absent households still had significantly higher odds of incarceration than those in mother-father families. Youth who never had a father in the home experienced the highest odds. A 2002 Department of Justice survey of 7,000 inmates revealed 39% of jail inmates lived in households where only a mother parented. Approximately 46% of jail inmates had a family member who had also been incarcerated. One-fifth experienced a father in prison or jail.
- **Discipline is another area where we see significant differences between mothers and fathers.** While women tend to be more sympathetic, fathers tend to be sterner. Fathers like to enforce the rules with an objective perspective, and this can instill in children a greater sense of right and wrong that can last a lifetime. Fathers also help boys develop self-respect for women and make girls more comfortable around men. These are two crucial aspects of a child's social development, especially in today's society in which gender equality and mutual respect are vital to success. (Liveabout.com 8-1-19).
- Finally, a recent research report has found that of those arrested and charged with murder in mass shootings, 84% were males from fatherless homes! (There are no female mass-shooters)

I must state emphatically that the above statistics relate to all cultures and races of people. This problem affects the entire population of this nation. Fathers are imperative. God knew what He was doing when He created men to be men, women to be women, and families to be families.

A Real-Life Example of a Godly Father

Let's go back to that incident of the young man I encountered at the convenience store that hot summer day years ago.

When the Holy Spirit spoke to me saying: "You don't know anything about this young man. You don't even know if he has a father!"

I was deeply convicted. I remembered asking God many times, "Why is my earthly family blessed as much as we are?" The Holy Spirit impressed me to examine the genealogy of both my father and my mother.

This concept was very unusual because I have never been interested in tracing my family history before. Nonetheless, I began to do some research, starting with my Daddy's side of the family.

My grandfather on my Dad's side died when I was very young. I could only remember one brief time with him when I was sitting in his lap in a chair on the front porch of his home.

He seemed at peace as he rocked me back and forth. At my later age as a teenager, I can remember hearing some of the older family members talking about my granddaddy and how "strange" he was.

Many years later, after my Daddy died, I visited my mother, who was then nearing her death. As we talked, I asked her about my grandfather McKinnon and referred to the comments I had heard from others many years ago.

I specifically asked if he had lost his mind and was a bit crazy. Mother laughed and said, "Heavens no! He was just in love with Jesus and had received the baptism of the Holy Spirit! His life changed drastically, and he began to witness to all who came into his store, leading many men and women to the Lord!"

This revelation was an awesome testimony of why my Daddy was the godly man he was as a father. As I continued to research, I learned many of my great grandfather's family members were devout Christians.

Next, I began to research my mother's family history. It was an amazing and powerful testimony of my mother's background being rooted and grounded in Christianity which she passed on to her children!

I eventually researched back in time to my great grandfather and discovered an amazing story of the power of prayer. His prayers continue to produce good fruit generations after his death.

William Jefferson Stewart was my great grandfather on my Mother's side of our family. He sold his farm in North Georgia in the early 1900s and moved his family to a rural community in South Georgia called Dixie (where I graduated from High School). He bought a farm there, and built a house on the farm where there was a large Live Oak tree in the back yard.

My mother was born in this house in 1909, and the large Live Oak tree continued to grow and still stands on that property. A few years ago, I measured the tree, and it measured twenty-eight feet in circumference. The family named the tree "The Prayer Tree" for a reason which will become evident as we continue.

My great grandfather had a hearing problem, so when he talked, he always spoke very loudly. Early every morning, as the sun rose, he would go outside and walk around under the big tree, praying in his loud voice.

Sounds travel a great distance in the early morning hours, and since he spoke loudly, the neighbors could hear his words clearly. My great grandfather would call the name of each of his children. He prayed for them that God would bless and protect them. He prayed they would fulfill His plan and purpose for them while on this earth.

When he finished praying for his children, he would begin to pray for those "yet to come" in generations that followed. Over the years since his passing, many men and women born of his lineage have entered the ministry and served in the kingdom of God. In my generation alone, there have been more than a dozen who have served as pastors of churches or other church-related positions.

My great grandfather is a powerful example of obedience to God's commandment for fathers to tell their children of His goodness and His works and their children to tell their children.

Consequently, this commandment results in a Christian linage that follows from generation to generation throughout life on this earth.

I have prayed in this manner under the same Prayer Tree every time I visit my family and friends in Dixie, Georgia. Additionally, every night when my wife and I go to bed, we pray over our children, their family members, and "all that will come in the generations of the future." We include, "even until Christ Jesus returns to this earth!"

What a blessing it is to us to observe our children and their children all serving the Lord.

Their lives are the manifest answers of Great Granddad's prayers as they live every day and serve in some form in their local churches.

My father in our earthly home fulfilled the requirements of a godly father in every aspect of his role. As I mentioned earlier, he was an extremely intelligent and gifted man who spent a great deal of his time managing the country store and the farm he owned. He would rise early in the morning and begin his duties during the day.

He raised his children to develop a work ethic that stayed with us throughout our lives. As a toddler, I carried firewood into the house to heat our home during the winter. At five years of age, I began milking cows every morning and afternoon. My mother used this milk to make butter and provide nutritious drinks for the family.

Other children in the family also had specific chores to complete daily. We were all paid for our work each week, and I can still remember each of us receiving a set of three tin cans that were to be used in a specific manner.

We were taught to put ten percent of our earnings in the can marked "Tithe." One of the other two cans was marked "Savings," and the third marked "spending." We were counseled on how to be good stewards of these three accounts.

Since my father worked every day from sunup to sundown, he didn't have much time to teach us the will and ways of God. My mother took the daily responsibility of doing this. However, my father lived this lifestyle by manifesting the will and ways of God in all he did. As stated earlier, he would frequently lead the Sunday school in the little country church where he was raised.

Dad was constantly teaching us how the Word of God was to be manifested in family life and our own lifestyle. We have followed his examples as guiding lights in our lives ever since.

God of Borders

As we read the Scriptures, we can see that God was a **God of Borders.** When the Israelites entered the Promised Land and had driven out its inhabitants, God gave the tribes of Israel their various properties – all clearly defined by borders he set for each tribe (See Joshua 15:1; 5-6; 12; 16:3; 5; 18:19).

Numerous Old Testament Scriptures verify that God establishes borders that are not to be violated. In the New Testament, Acts records, *"And He has made from one blood every nation of men to dwell on all the face of the earth, and has determined their pre-appointed times and the **boundaries** of their dwellings"* (Acts 17:26).

My earthly father was a man of borders. He had standards that were not to be violated.

We didn't miss Sunday church services. When we did our work responsibilities, they must be done according to his schedule and instructions. When we played baseball, basketball, football, etc., we gave it our all and played by the rules.

As we grew older and began to date, he and my mother approved our choice of dates and were assigned a certain time to return home.

Of course, certain boundaries were set concerning how we conducted ourselves on these dates. We were taught to open the car door and help the lady in and out of the car. We must, by all means, be "gentlemen" in the way we treated our dates!

Furthermore, he trained us up by setting boundaries on how we communicated with people. Everyone who was an adult we addressed as "Mr" or "Miss" or "Mrs."

We were always taught to remove our caps or hats when entering a home, office, or other professional institution.

Daddy was most specific about honoring authorities. I'll never forget his instructions. He taught us that two things could hurt us – a pencil and a pistol. Daddy said that teachers, employers, and others in positions of authority had a pencil and that law enforcement personnel had both a pencil and a pistol.

This insight helped me avoid a lot of problems in my life. I assure you I have never argued with a law enforcement officer and have always honored their authority. Authority is created and authorized by God our Creator, whether we approve of it or not.

Romans 13:1-3 records: *"Let every soul be subject to the governing authorities. For there is no authority except from God, and the authorities that exist are appointed by God. Therefore, whoever resists the authority resists the ordinance of God, and those who resist will bring judgment on themselves. For rulers are not a terror to good works, but to evil. Do you want to be unafraid of the authorities? Do what is good, and you will have praise from the same."*

Dad also had borders for when money was available and not available for something we wanted to purchase. He gave all his children some of the best counsel I've ever heard concerning financial matters.

It was very simple - if funds were needed for some purchase that was essential for making more money, it was fine to borrow money on the item to produce enough extra income to pay off the loan.

Never borrow money for something you just want. Instead, save up the money required for the purchase and then pay cash for it.

This wisdom is confirmed in the Holy Scriptures. God states in Proverbs 22:7. *"The rich rules over the poor, and the borrower is servant to the lender."* (See also Proverbs 18:23 and James 2:5-7). Oh, how I wish I had listened to and applied his counsel in my business dealings years later!

I am keenly aware of the mindset of parents of children these days as it relates to the discipline of their children. In today's culture, many parents absolutely refuse to physically punish their children with what is commonly called spanking.

In the Scriptures, this word is often 'chastening.' Of course, *chastening* can often be produced by spoken words. However, a brief review of the Scriptures reveals physical chastening is sometimes required.

In Proverbs, King Solomon wrote: *"He who spares the rod hates his son, but he who loves him disciplines him promptly"* (Proverbs 13:24). In Proverbs 22:15, he adds: *"Foolishness is bound up in the heart of a child; the rod of correction will drive it far from him."* For other references, see Proverbs 29:15 or Hebrews 12:4-11.

My Daddy never physically abused us, but we were corrected by a 'switch' or his belt when we violated the behavioral boundaries he had established.

Now we were not dumb or ignorant - we were just normal children who frequently tested the boundaries. It didn't take us long to learn some of our thoughts or plans were out of bounds, and we knew punishment was to follow.

We soon learned to watch his face and know when we were about to cross the line. One quick look and we abandoned our ill-conceived plan. Our earthly father was a man of God who raised his children in accordance with the word of God, and we respected him highly.

I'll never forget the night he died. He was only 75 years old at the time, but through a series of physical problems, he wound up in the ICU unit at the Emory University hospital, where he stayed for six weeks.

As time drew near for his journey to his heavenly home, my brothers and I stayed with our mother and dad twenty-four hours a day. In the middle of the night, his nurse woke me, as I had asked her to, and told me there had been a final change and our Dad was at death's door. He had been in a coma the biggest part of the week and was in that condition when my mother, my adopted brother, and I entered his room.

I had seen so many different expressions on his face over the years - anger at sinful living, amazement over a birthday or Christmas gift he was not expecting, sorrow over a loved one's death, or compassion and love he was feeling. This time was different. I didn't recognize this look.

Suddenly, Dad's eyes opened. He apparently was not even aware of us standing over him but was looking straight up with his face revealing he was staring straight into something so awesome it could not be described! This lasted but a few seconds before he closed his eyes and slipped into the presence of the Lord forever!

The three of us in the room immediately raised our hands in the air and began to praise God. This was His gift to us, His goodness on our behalf.

It was obvious that the nurses watching over us had never seen such a sight in their entire career.

As I think of my earthly Father and how blessed I was to be a part of his family, I can summarize his life on the earth best by referring to a particular account recorded in the Old Testament. The event runs from the 6th through the 8th chapters of Judges.

The 6th chapter begins by pointing out that the Israelites did evil in the sight of the Lord, so the Lord delivered them into the hand of Midian for seven years.

The summary reads, *"The Midianites would come up with their livestock and their tents, coming in as numerous as locusts; both they and their camels were without number, and they would enter the land to destroy it. So, the Israelites were greatly impoverished because of the Midianites, and the children of Israel cried out to the Lord."*

The Lord heard their cry and sent an Angel to confront a man named Gideon, saying to him, *"The Lord is with you, you mighty man of valor!"*

Basically, the Lord ordained Gideon to gather the men of battle and go to war against the Midianites. We read that there were about 32,000 men able to go to war. However, after a time of testing, only 300 men were deemed fit by the Lord. Twenty-two thousand were fearful, so they were dismissed. The story demonstrates that God needs men who are courageous and do His will His way.

Through a series of events, the Lord gave Gideon instructions. Soon, Gideon and the three hundred men stood overlooking the Midianites as they prepared to retire for the night.

Gideon divided the three hundred men into three companies, and he assigned each man a trumpet, an empty pitcher, and a torch inside the pitcher. He then gave them instructions about what to do with these odd 'weapons' of war. *"Look at me and do likewise; watch, and when I come to the edge of the camp, do as I do"* (Judges 7:17).

I conclude the coverage of this event with this awesome and spiritually powerful 21st verse: **"And every man <u>stood in his place</u> all around the camp, and the whole army (of the Midianites) *ran and cried out and fled."*** What an amazing and powerful spiritual illustration of courage and obedience!

What is the point about my earthly Daddy? He was always a man who **"stood in his place"** as an earthly father. My heart grieves for those who don't have fathers with this heart and mindset. I am sure many godly men in this nation have taken their place and raised or are raising their children according to the pattern and plan of God. I only wish there were more.

The Mark Richt Story

I would be remiss if I did not share with you one more man who has manifested such a lifestyle in an amazing and heartwarming manner. I have never personally met this awesome man, but I have followed his life last fifty or sixty years. He has greatly impacted my life.

I first observed him in the early years of my thirty-one-year career with the University of Georgia Cooperative Extension Service. I graduated from the University of Georgia with a bachelor's degree and began my career in Crisp County, Georgia. I have always loved football and have always been a fanatic over the Georgia Bulldogs football team. Go Dawgs!

My wife and our young family attended many of the Bulldog's games in Athens, Georgia. At each game, the team would take the field for their pre-game exercise regimen. What impressed me most was when I watched coach Richt walk among the players and place his hand each one. I later found out he was praying over them.

Coach Richt served as the Bulldog's head coach from 2001-2015. During his tenure as head coach, the Bulldogs won two Southeastern Conference championships, six SEC Eastern Division titles, and nine bowl games. His team represented the SEC in three BCS bowl appearances with a record of 2-1 and finished in the top ten of the coaches' poll. He later returned to his Alma mater, the University of Miami, where he coached until his retirement in 2018.

Once each year, the UGA Extension Service where I worked held an annual meeting somewhere in the State, and all employees were expected to attend. In 2001, the annual meeting was held at the Georgia 4-H Club Center in Eatonton, Georgia. The meeting began, and they introduced the guest speaker, Mr. Mark Richt, the new head coach of the Georgia Bulldogs.

I was excited and awestruck that Mark was the keynote speaker. His talk to us that day was one of the most challenging and edifying speeches I believe I've ever heard.

Coach Richt is married to Katharyn Francis of Tallahassee, Florida. The couple has four children: Jonathan, David, and two children they adopted from Ukraine in 1999, Anya and Zach. Anya was born with a rare disorder known as Proteus Syndrome.

His son Jonathan worked under Coach Richt as the quarterback coach for the Miami Hurricanes. Based on what I've seen from a distance, from what I've read or heard through the media, and what I have found out through detailed research, Coach Richt is indeed a godly man and a devout Christian, and his staff has always been a mix of religious backgrounds.

Arthur Lynch, a member of the 2013 UGA team, posted this on Facebook in December 2018: "Now that he is retired, I don't think CMR (Coach Mark Richt) will mind me sharing this story that perfectly illustrates who he is as a football coach, and more importantly, as a man.

It was January of 2011; we had just finished the season 6-7 with a loss to UCF in the Liberty Bowl. CMR called a team meeting, which wasn't abnormal during that time of year, as we usually met as a team before the second semester to go over classes, workouts, goals, etc.

However, this meeting was surrounded by rumors that Coach Richt was offered another coaching job - for more money at his alma mater, and we believed he was going to take it. Obviously, we wouldn't have blamed him due to the pressures of coaching in the SEC and the fact that he was on the 'hot seat.'

As we sat down, a single chair was in front of the team meeting room, which we all knew to be the hot seat usually set up during the preseason. For those unfamiliar, the hot seat is an opportunity for any member of the program to get in front of the team and share his personal story. Mainly meant for seniors, others have sat there before, and that day was Coach Richt's turn to speak his truth.

We were expecting his farewell, but what we were given was the most revealing and telling depiction of who Coach Richt truly was as a man.

He explained that he wanted nothing more than winning a championship and finishing his job here at Georgia but believed it wasn't his sole purpose. His purpose was to raise each of us as if we were his own and fulfill the promises he made to our parents and loved ones."

Mark Richt is not perfect, but he represents the characteristics I saw in my father and read about in Gideon.

Mark stood in the place God called him to, and he took a personal interest in each man who played for his teams over the years. He represented his institutions and Christ well and made a profound impact on many young men.

Some of them went on to play in the NFL, but most of them are just men and dads and employers and employees. All of them carry the lessons learned in those games; more importantly, they carry those prayers of Mark Richt.

God, the Creator

My wife Ginger and I are definitely not – nor have we ever had jobs – in the high-income bracket. However, we have diligently set aside a little money throughout the year to enable us to take a vacation to the beach each year.

We found a place on Okaloosa Island on the Gulf Coast of Florida. We really enjoy going for two weeks early every summer. We usually rent a condo on the sixth floor, which has a nice balcony that overlooks the beach and the ocean.

A few years ago, our daughter Susan and her husband Joe Kerr joined us for a few days. It was a great time together. Late one afternoon, we were sitting on the balcony and talking about the beauty of the ocean and the never-ending waves that pounded back and forth. I began to wonder how deep the deepest place of the sea was, so we began to do some research on the matter. What we discovered was astounding!

The Mariana Trench is the deepest point in Earth's oceans. The trench is located in the western North Pacific Ocean. The ocean floor there is 10,924 meters (35,840 feet) deep. To get an idea of just how deep that is, if Mount Everest - the highest mountain on Earth - were placed upside down in the trench, it would be over a mile deep underwater!

The deep waters create intense pressure. At the lowest depths, the pressure reaches over 17,750 pounds per square inch! That's more than a thousand times the atmospheric pressure at sea level on land. Most creatures would literally be crushed flat at that depth under that pressure.

No sunlight penetrates to that depth, so any organism that requires photosynthesis to exist cannot live in the trench. The average temperature is barely above freezing, reaching 1 degree Celsius, about 34 degrees Fahrenheit. Technically, nothing should live there, and yet researchers discovered life is thriving there!

With absolutely no sunlight penetrating to that depth, there is no photosynthesis—organisms converting light into food. Instead, there is a unique process of chemosynthesis that creates food by converting inorganic molecules into organic compounds. These compounds are then consumed by bacteria, crustaceans, octopus, fish, shrimp, and numerous creatures.

These deep-sea dwellers live near searing hot springs that belch up sulfuric gases charged by undersea volcanic activity deep inside the earth.

At that depth, under that pressure, in toxic hyper-heated water, nothing should be able to live. Yet in these impossible conditions, God has placed creatures that live to exhibit His creativity and miracle power nearly 7 miles below sea level!

If God would go to those depths to show His majesty, in a place we will never see, how far would that amazing Creator God go to demonstrate His love and power in our lives?

My heart grieves for those who believe there is no God.

The very word of God testifies of this where it is written: *"For the wrath of God is revealed from heaven against all ungodliness and unrighteousness of men, who suppress the truth in unrighteousness, because what may be known of God is manifest in them, for God has shown it to them. For since the creation of the world, His invisible attributes are clearly seen, being understood by the things that are made, even His eternal power and Godhead (divine nature and deity), so that they are without excuse, because, although they knew God, they did not glorify Him as God, nor were thankful, but became futile in their thoughts, and their foolish hearts were darkened"* (Romans 1:18-21).

I have always been an avid hunter and fisherman. I remember quite well after I was saved how I was so much in love with Jesus Christ, my Savior and the Lord of my life. Whether fishing on the Ocmulgee River or a beautiful lake or hunting from twenty feet high up a tree in the woods, I enjoy the time alone with God.

I thoroughly enjoy watching the light of the sun rising early in the morning. It reminds me that in the kingdom, light always displaces darkness.

I was always overcome with amazement and awe to be in the presence of God, the Creator. I recall sitting in a deer stand when all was quiet, the sun just rising. Suddenly I was aware of the sound of wings behind me. As I turned around, I observed a beautiful turkey that had just left his roost and flown to a fallen tree right behind me.

Again, amazement overcame me as I watched this beautiful wild bird that God has made. It was sitting within ten feet of me, unaware of my presence. I have observed bobcats, foxes, raccoons, and other wild animals moving through the forest at that time in similar conditions.

My heart is burdened for those poor unenlightened souls who deny the existence of God and His creation. The eternal, absolute truth is, a day is coming when *"all people will bow, of those* *in heaven, and those on earth, and those under the earth, and that every tongue should confess that Jesus Christ is Lord, to the glory of the Father"* (Philippians 2:10-11). One day, every person will be on their knees before Jesus Christ and acknowledge Him as Lord.

There is a sad truth for the people who have rejected Jesus Christ all their life. Their confession that He is Lord will come too late, and they will be disallowed to enter God's heaven and instead be assigned to eternity in hell!

I plead with anyone who is reading this and has not repented and asked Jesus to forgive them - invite Jesus Christ to come into their heart and be the Lord of your life! Jesus Himself has stated: *"I am the way, the truth, and the life.* **No one comes to the Father except through Me***"* (John 14:6).

A Return to the First Wrestling Match

At some point during this time in His holy presence, the Lord gave me a "flashback" to when I was just a small boy. It was during the middle of the 2nd world war, and all things were very limited. We were issued coupons that were limited only for a short time and were to be used only to purchase food supplies.

I remembered seeing a drawing in the local newspaper, which showed this young boy standing and reading a notice posted on the door of the school's dining hall. Before these days, milk was furnished to all students. However, the notice read: "Milk. Five cents per glass."

This young boy was barefooted and dressed in old, frayed overalls, and he had pulled out his front pocket, holding it out to see that no money was there. The caption showed the young boy saying, "Shucks, I wasn't hungry anyway."

As a young lad myself, I felt so sad for this young man. I clipped the drawing out and put it in my wallet. I would frequently take it out, look at it, and again become very upset over this injustice!

I kept this article until it simply wore out and began to fall to pieces. As the Lord showed me this incident in my life, He spoke to me and said, "My son, what I have just reminded you of was the depth of compassion I put in your heart when I was creating you before time began. Over the years, you have allowed your heart to become hardened! With My calling upon you, which you have now received and accepted, I am softening your heart to restore this compassion, for it is to become a vital part of your calling in the ministry!"

I recalled many times in the New Testament that Jesus, while on this earth, "was moved with compassion" when He observed people in need.

Since that time, I have been diligent in keeping a heart of compassion at the center of ministering to others, no matter their situation.

The Pattern Hidden and Covered

The **Pattern** of God is a reflection of His nature. He is pure, holy, and uncompromising. Pattern represents everything we understand about God and how His Kingdom functions: He is reliable, trustworthy, unflinching, and absolute.

Satan and his kingdom are the opposite of God's Pattern and Plan. Reflecting his pride and arrogance, Satan deceives, destroys, and defiles. In our current day, the mindset of Individualism has corrupted God's principle of Pattern.

In the early years of my career as a County Extension Agent, we regularly hosted meetings for farmers, livestock owners, landscaping projects, small business management, and others.

The resources came from what we called 'Specialists' stationed either in Athens or Tifton, Georgia. These Specialists were men or women professionals in the areas mentioned above. They kept updated on the latest research projects. This was no small task given the many research scientists stationed at several research facilities in Georgia.

During our meetings with farmers and other groups, we would call in the Specialists to help us conduct training seminars with the latest research.

In these early days, we used overhead projectors to display the visual elements of the research presentations. Many reading this book probably are not familiar with this equipment since it has been replaced with more high-tech equipment like digital slide stacks, DVDs, or videos.

Overhead projectors used sheets of transparent plastic film placed on the projector's flat glass screen. A light under this flat screen shined up through the glass and the transparency film.

Whatever you wrote on the film would be projected and magnified through a lens above the screen and then angled to display on the wall.

The Specialist in charge could change the film or write on the film to advance the presentation or illustrate a point. The projection to the screen was very sharp and clear with the first film or two.

A new piece of film, which presented the next step in the discussion, could be placed on top of the original. Additional films were added, and with each new sheet, the original film was slowly buried deeper in the stack.

As the presentation progressed, the stack of films would grow thicker or the original sheet would be erased and rewritten, each time leaving a little ink smudge remaining. The original film would be written on repeatedly or covered in piles of sheets until the original became buried or smeared until it was unreadable.

That's exactly what has happened as our Individualism society has grown. The eternal truth of God has been "covered over." This is precisely what Satan, the enemy of God, has very subtly done to cover over God's original Pattern.

In the Book of Ezekiel, the prophet writes about how Satan, who wanted to replace God and His kingdom. Satan used the gifting God had bestowed on him to corrupt and "cover over" the **pattern** for God's kingdom and His household.

Ezekiel records Satan's attempt to become God and details how God punished Satan. Ezekiel explains it was Satan's pride and rebellion that caused him to be cast out of heaven.

Ezekiel records, *"You were the anointed cherub **who covers**; I established you; you were on the holy mountain of God; You walked back and forth in the midst of fiery stones. You were perfect in your ways from the day you were created till iniquity was found in you. By the abundance of your pride, you became filled with violence, and you sinned; Therefore, I cast you as a profane thing out of the mountain of God; And I destroyed you, O **covering** cherub from the midst of the fiery stones."* (Ezekiel 28:14-16).

Not only has Satan, the enemy of God, covered over God's pattern for His Household, he has covered God's pattern and plan for our human society and Government.

I fully believe that God had a strong hand in the founding father's lives as they began to create our system of government. God's influence created the pattern or plan for this nation just as surely as He has established others before it.

I distinctly remember when I was young and beginning school. The very first thing each day, the principal would call every class, from first grade to the senior class, into the school's auditorium. We would begin the assembly with prayer and Scripture reading. The next thing on the agenda was to repeat together the Pledge of Allegiance. All of us were required to place our right hands on our hearts as we pledged allegiance to the flag. After this was done, we had the day's announcements, and then we were dismissed to begin our day's schooling.

What a sad difference in the culture of the days we now live: prayer and Bible teaching are not allowed in most school systems today. In some, the

Pledge of Allegiance is not allowed! The same holds true in some courtrooms - the only exception is the Bible's use to swear in those called to testify in a trial.

I often wonder about the history books students learn from today. Have they been rewritten and smeared and covered with layers of opinion and misinformation? Do they contain any focus at all on the **Pattern** God gave the founding fathers when this awesome nation was founded?

A quote attributed to writer and philosopher George Santayana states: "Those who do not learn from history are doomed to repeat it." Those who cannot remember the past or were not taught the past are likely to repeat its mistakes.

It seems that as a result of the Individualism culture, our nation is in the process of repeating the rise and fall of nations before us.

Why do I say this? Jesus stated it simply and firmly to the Pharisees in Matthew's Gospel. He identified reason any nation falls—division. *"But Jesus knew their thoughts, and said to them, 'Every kingdom divided against itself is brought to desolation, and every city or house divided against itself will not stand!'"* (Matthew 12:25)

I have never in my whole life seen such a nation divided against itself as I observe in America today. Corruption and pride are deep and dark in almost every area of government, from the lowest levels to top leadership in the Capitol. The same thing is taking place in state and local governments across the nation.

We have reviewed statistics and evidence from recent research that substantiates this concept. First there is division, then comes destruction. Where we are now in that process is only known to

God, but we have been given a glimpse of His Plan and Pattern and we must do our part in this time.

God is a God of Order, and He hates disorder and confusion. On the other hand, God loves unity. This concept is detailed many places in the Holy Scriptures. We will look at three instances which illustrate God's reaction to disunity and His promise to those who are unified.

Let's examine first God's response to a united people, but people who were using their unity in an attempt to do something contrary to the will of God.

This event followed the action of a people who were descendants of the family of Noah. They had survived the flood that destroyed all living creatures on the earth. Only those in the ark survived. In Genesis chapter 11, we see that the whole earth had one language and one speech at that time.

They all came together and decided to build a city for themselves with a tower whose top allowed them to worship the heavens, not the God of the heavens, but the moon and stars themselves.

The Bible tells us the Lord came down to see the city and the tower, which the sons of men had built. *"And the Lord said, 'Indeed the people **are one**, and they all have one language, and this is what they begin to do; **now nothing that they to do will be withheld from them.**"*

As a result of this misguided judgment, God *"went down and confused their language, that they might not understand one another's speech."* The results? In verse eight, we read: *"So the Lord scattered them abroad from there over the face of the earth, and they ceased building the city."*

The Household of God

You might wonder why God would do this to people who were unified in their thinking. The answer is found at the beginning of creation, recorded in the first chapter of Genesis. God's purpose and plan for humanity are made quite clear when He created man and woman.

Genesis 1:8 tells us, *"Then God blessed them, and God said to them, "Be fruitful and multiply; fill the earth and subdue it; have dominion over the fish of the sea, over the birds of the air, and over every living thing that moves on the earth."* Simply put, they were disobedient to God and violated His commandments.

In the book of the Prophet Amos, Chapter 3, verse 3, the prophet asks a series of questions – all with the implied answer, **"NO."** *Can two walk together unless they are agreed?"*

Now let's examine the benefits of agreement that our covenant God provides. King David wrote Psalm 133. We will focus on David's message in the first three verses. David writes,

*"Behold, how good and how pleasant it is for brethren to dwell together in **unity**! It is like the precious oil upon the head, running down on the beard, the beard of Aaron, running down on the edge of his garments. It is like the dew of Hermon, descending upon the mountains of Zion; For there the Lord **commanded the blessing - life forevermore.**"*

Let this sink deep into your heart and mind! Notice this first, *"For there the Lord commanded the blessing - Life evermore..."* refers to the first verse where the Psalmist is speaking of **"brethren together in unity!!!**

This is an excellent example of how God's commandments work. When obeyed, they allow our awesome loving covenant God to fulfill His covenant - He proves His promise of unity.

As far as our nation is concerned, we are anything but unified; rather, we are about as un-unified as a nation can get. How can God bless that?

I urge you to review for yourself the stories about the founding fathers. A good resource is the organization, Wall Builders which you can find online. They have a massive library of historical documents and biblical references from the founding fathers of this country – over 100,000 letters and books and writings that prove beyond any doubt that God's hand was at work establishing this country.

The Holy Spirit's guidance formed this nation as those men followed God's Word. The foresight and wisdom they demonstrated in writing the Constitution and the Bill of Rights simply had to come from the wisdom of God through the Holy Spirit!

Would God go to that much effort to lay such a foundation and build this country to have it dismantled and destroyed in a generation? I don't think so. God's Pattern and Plan and Household are eternal. His foundation is trustworthy and sure. It may seem shaky now, but God is the Head of this Household, and He will lead us if we will follow.

The Conclusion of the Whole Matter

I pray for our nation. I intercede for our President and for our judges and senators and our military leaders. As we saw in the early days of this nation, the word from God and the prayers of His people can bring about great change.

God loves the world. 1 Peter 3:9 tells us that *"God is not willing that any should perish."* He stands ready to deliver, to heal, to restore, and to forgive. I do not know if there is revival ahead for our nation or if there is judgment, but I know God's heart is to love and save and deliver.

We cannot control what the government does, but we can do our part and vote and speak up and live a godly life. We cannot unite people deeply divided over the many issues that confront our country, but we can speak like Jesus and act like Jesus to one person today.

We can say yes to God's Pattern and Plan in our individual lives. We can live out God's will and purpose in our family. We can be the part of the Body of Christ that we are each called to be.

The Body is not unified because we are all the same; it is unified because we are all different, but we each perform the function we are called to do. We fulfill God's Plan when we use the gifts He has given to do what He has called us to do.

We fulfill God's Plan when we align our hearts and our work with His eternal will. It is a daily decision, a moment-by-moment choice to conform to His Pattern, and live out His Plan.

We are His workmanship, created in Christ Jesus. We demonstrate His Pattern when we look and sound and act like Christ. We fulfill His Plan when we continue to conform to His Pattern each time we make another choice. The Pattern is the result of following the Plan one step at a time.

Just like the foundation we discussed earlier, the blueprints detail the larger Plan. The Pattern is how we get there – one building block at a time. We may not change the country, then again, maybe we will. It wouldn't be the first time in history God sent the sweet rain of revival and withheld judgment.

That is up to God because only He knows the entire Pattern and Plan. Our part is to live by the Pattern, and apply the Plan each day.

What is God's Pattern and Plan for your life? His ultimate plan is for you to spend eternity with Him in heaven. If you have never made that decision, do it right now. Trust Him with your life and give Him your heart. Become a member of the eternal Household of God.

Next, begin building the Household of God on this earth – one building block at a time. Begin with your family, your work, your relationships. Apply the principles we outlined in this book and build upon the eternal Cornerstone, Christ Jesus.

A household built on His solid foundation will withstand the storms of life. Pray for our nation that God gives us time and repentance to revival and restoration. Live unto Christ.

Face today and tomorrow as Hebrews tells us Abraham lived: *"...he waited for the city which has foundations, whose builder and maker is God"* (Hebrews 11:10). He is both the builder and Chief Cornerstone of the Household of God.

www.ingramcontent.com/pod-product-compliance
Lightning Source LLC
Chambersburg PA
CBHW031251290426
44109CB00012B/531